Worthy Caws

A year of healing and communing with crows

Katie Brotten

Worthy Caws
A year of healing and communing with crows

No part of this publication may be reproduced in whole or in part, or stored in a retrieval system, or transmitted in any form or by any means, electronic, mechanical, photocopying, or otherwise, without the written permission of the publisher, except in the case of brief quotations embodied in critical reviews and certain other uses permitted by copyright law.

To request permission, or for any other information about this publication, please email katiebrotten@gmail.com.

Copyright © 2024 Katie Brotten

All photographs taken by Katie Brotten unless otherwise labeled.

All rights reserved.

Paperback Edition ISBN: 9798323160020

To both of my grandmothers.

One who asked me, just a couple weeks after my first book was published, "That was so good! So… when are you publishing your next book?" Talk about keeping me on track! This is for you.

And to my other grandmother who comforted me after I'd inadvertently watched Hitchcock's movie, "The Birds" at a too-young age to be watching such a thing. I lost my fear of the movie (now one of my favorites) and my fear of crows because of our conversation.

WORTHY CAWS

CONTENTS

	Acknowledgments	i
	Introduction	3
1	Vinnie and his Crow Friends	5
2	Walking as Meditation, Walking as Healing	15
3	"Your Order Has Arrived"	25
4	The Start of the Crows	29
5	Shenanigans	35
6	Tell your crows I said hello	47
7	A Sense of Humor	51
8	The Introvert's Dilemma	55
9	Gifts	59
10	The R-Rated Movie	61
11	Goofing Off	67
12	More Snacks!	71
13	Conversations with Crows	83
14	Murder Me	91
15	Visitors	99
16	10,000 Bodyguards	107
17	2,000 Photographs	111
18	I Met Them at the Bar, and then We Played Hide & Seek	113
19	Love is Never Wasted	115
	Conclusion	117

ACKNOWLEDGMENTS

I have the best people in my life, and so many people to thank… not only for this book, but for encouraging me in different activities and arenas of my life.

Whenever I have an interest in something, my friends and family are immediately onboard. With my dog Vinnie, with my writing, with crows. As soon as I started posting crow pictures on social media, my buddies sent me crow videos, memes, interesting crow facts. Thank you to all of you who asked about my crow friends and said, "Tell your crows I said hello."

Thank you to everyone who has encouraged me, given me feedback, and complimented my writing. I've been writing for so long, ever since I was 4 years old and had a little pink and yellow journal. At that age, all I knew how to write was my name in big block letters. Ever since then, writing has been a daily activity for me, and because of the quotidian nature of it, I sometimes forget that I actually have something important and worthwhile to say. I write because I *need* to write, almost as much as I need to breathe, and when people take the time to tell me how much they enjoy my essays and vignettes and funny anecdotes, it means a lot to me. Your kind words lift me up.

Thank you to my beta readers: Mary Rollins, Catherine Pierce, Bob Riley! So helpful to get that feedback and boost of confidence before publishing!

Thank you to the many of you who provided feedback with the title and the cover. This was such a team effort!

Thank you to all of you who supported my first book about my beloved Vinnie, my yellow lab mix of 13 years. It was such a healing journey to write that book after he and I said goodbye… goodbye for now, at least.

And thank you to Vinnie. Grieving you was the most difficult thing I have ever done, and the process of my grief led me to meditative, healing walks… which led me to the crows and to writing this book. Thank you for being my best friend and for all the walks and swims we took together. Thanks for your gentleness with me, with people and other animals, and with our crow friends.

Introduction

The year 2023 was extremely difficult for me. I lost my dog Vinnie in February; he was the love of my life, my first dog I had as an adult, and we did everything together during his long and happy life of 13 years.

After Vinnie passed away, I started walking several miles every day. He and I hadn't gone on many long walks during his last year because of his physical limitations. Getting back into long walks was a great way for me to get exercise, as well as reminisce about the long hikes and treks we were able to take together.

Some days I didn't walk much, maybe a mile or two. On other days, I walked 13 or 14 miles. I started feeding crows on my walks, and again, the numbers varied; sometimes I saw only a crow or two, and other times I saw thousands upon thousands, a veritable murder of crows swooping down towards me. And with each walk, each crow interaction, I started to heal from my grief over Vinnie.

As I was healing, I began to appreciate the relationships I was building with the crows. They made me laugh, they seemed happy and excited to see me, and I loved seeing them as well. My crows became a consistent source of connection; I knew that there would be at least one or two crows I could interact with each and every day, and it would be an interaction of mutual admiration and respect.

This book is a collection of essays, encounters, and pictures from my year of walking with crows. During my walks, I learned a lot about crows, interspecies communication, and different ways of healing. I also learned a lot about myself, my community, and the importance of animals in our world. These were important lessons that will stay with me for the rest of my life.

Vinnie and his Crow Friends

In his younger years, Vinnie and I walked all the time. We lived in the same small town for 11 years, we knew every crack in every sidewalk, every hidden pathway, and the best places to swim and run and hike. Many times, we walked from our town to the next town over and then back again, walking 8 or 10 miles in a single day. That first decade or more of his life, he had so much energy, and these longs walks helped us manage that energy. It helped me too; I tend to be high-strung as my default setting, and so being outdoors and exercising was win-win.

Our favorite walk was along a trail that is parallel to a river, and throughout the walk, Vinnie would periodically jump into the water to cool off. He lapped up the river water, splashed around, and had so much fun. He loved to swim more than any other activity, and I loved watching him swim. I took him swimming almost every day of his life, and often to a couple of different places in a single day, especially during the Summer months. One of the perks of living in the Seattle area is being surrounded by the ocean, lakes, and rivers.

Ever since his puppy years, I instructed him to "Leave the birds." There is a reason for this which I will get into later, but this instruction included leaving the birds, ducks, geese, and chickens alone. He learned quickly and we never had any issues with this.

However, not wanting him to completely deny his hunting-dog instincts, I did allow him to chase the squirrels, knowing he could never catch them before they escaped up a tree. Vinnie was too gentle to hurt anyone anyway; one day he caught a bunny, but "caught" isn't even the right word. He didn't put his mouth on him but sort of cornered him against a tree and then sniffed the bunny's neck out of sheer curiosity for a few seconds. The bunny, probably confused by Vinnie's gentle, non-violent behavior, stood there for a few seconds, and then he simply hopped away. Vinnie didn't chase after him, but just smiled like he'd made a new friend.

Vinnie was so gentle as his default setting, and with birds he often didn't even make eye contact with them. This was great, because then they were never scared of him. Vinnie and birds all just co-existed peacefully for Vinnie's entire life.

Vinnie's first crow encounter

One day, I had some leftover popcorn in my car from going to the movies earlier that afternoon. I tossed a few kernels onto the sidewalk outside of my house for the few crows that were hanging out in the trees above me, and then I walked up the stairs to grab Vinnie for a little stroll. When he and I walked back outside, the crows were clustered around the popcorn.

"Oh, do you like popcorn? I actually wasn't sure if crows ate popcorn."

When Vinnie saw the crows, he didn't pester them. He did put his nose in the air, though, maybe catching a whiff of buttery popcorn. Labradors will eat anything, and Vinnie often did.

"We are going to walk this way," I told Vinnie. "We gotta give the birds some space."

When the crows saw me that day with non-intimidating Vinnie, they didn't even flinch. They were used to seeing us go in and out of the front door all day long, to and from walks and adventures.

After that initial popcorn sampling, we started bringing snacks on our walks in case we had more chances to interact with crows. And almost every day, the crows would fly over to us when we left the house and I would toss them the snacks.

"This is the bird's food, okay, Vinnie? Not for you. Bird treats."

Vinnie seemed to understand; he was so smart. I always spoke to him in complete sentences, and I think that is why he and I understood each other so well throughout his life. When I fed the crows, he wouldn't even attempt to eat or even reach for the little snacks.

Vinnie's crows seemed to like him, or at least didn't seem bothered by him at all. They even continued following us on our walks after they'd eaten all the treats. The first time they did this, I assumed they wanted more treats, but when I tossed more down that were then ignored, I realized maybe something else was going on. They flew from tree to tree, looking down at us silently. I enjoyed their company, and Vinnie probably did, too; crows are social birds, and Vinnie was social too, always the life of the party. The crows even spent time with us at the park sometimes, rooting around in the grass for snacks while Vinnie and I relaxed on a nearby blanket by the river.

"Good boy. Those are your crow *friends*!"

At this word, Vinnie would usually look up at me and smile. When he was a puppy, I taught him the word, "friend," and we used it to describe his human buddies, animal friends, and non-living but potentially scary objects like vacuums and fireworks. I even used this word for not-particularly scary objects like plastic bags and unfamiliar objects (one year's Christmas tree stand comes to mind, as he growled at it sitting innocently in the corner). As soon as he learned these things were "friends," his wariness disappeared. Helping him associate the word "friend" with positive things was probably the smartest thing I did with him.

The only time he was scared around a bird was during an encounter in his younger years; but in this instance, I was scared, too. On this particular evening, we were walking on our favorite trail alongside the river. We were in a shady part, walking through a path lined by tall trees that filtered the soft light of the setting sun.

Suddenly, we saw an eagle soaring over us. As we stood there, we watched as the eagle descended lower and lower to the ground, closer and closer to the trail we were standing on.

"What?" I said aloud, wondering what was going on.

Vinnie started to breathe more heavily, panting and jumping around. His eyes were worriedly fixed on the eagle.

I started to wonder if the eagle was going to grab Vinnie. But that was impossible, right? Vinnie was at least 60 pounds at this point. The eagle couldn't possibly think he could carry him off... right?

Finally, the eagle swooped down and landed in the grass next to us, about 10 feet away. I thought he was dive-bombing us. But then I saw him pick up something from the ground, a tiny already-deceased wild animal that was lying in the grass. It was the same small critter that Vinnie and I had seen a few seconds earlier on our walk, which I had promptly forgotten about in my own fight-or-flight mode.

I had never been that close to an eagle before. They are huge and intimidating, and beautiful.

As the eagle flew off, he was chased by 2 crows. I didn't even have a chance to grab my camera to capture the exciting scene.

(•ᵥ•)   (•ᵥ•)   (•ᵥ•)

Other than the occasional scare, Vinnie's love for all animals was consistent. His respect for eagles and crows translated to other birds throughout our adventures together.

In 2021, Vinnie and I moved onto a boat and lived there for 8 months. We moved onto the boat in February of that year, and a few weeks later during the height of Spring, several ducks started swimming by to check us out.

"Do you want to give the ducks some food?" I asked Vinnie.

He looked up at me and smiled. I took that as a "yes," and tossed the ducks some of his dog food. They loved it.

One day, a male and female duck jumped up onto the boat dock where Vinnie was standing. He looked at them with wonder; and in his typical extroverted Labrador behavior, approached them, albeit slowly.

Suddenly, the male duck reached out his beak and bit Vinnie on the nose. Vinnie immediately stepped backwards, licked his nose, and then looked up at me embarrassedly, like he felt he had done something wrong.

"It's okay; he was just scared. Those are your duck friends," I tried to reassure him.

After that first act of duck-initiated violence, there were no other issues between Vinnie and his duck friends. The ducks, both the males and the females, seemed to realize Vinnie was chill and cool. By the end of March and early April, mother ducks brought their baby ducklings by the boat to visit us. Vinnie continued to share his food, and on at least one occasion, a mother duck brought her babies up on board the boat to take a little nap on Vinnie's comfy dog bed. Vinnie was always generous and great at sharing.

(•ᵥ•) (•ᵥ•) (•ᵥ•)

After 13.3 years, it was time for me to say goodbye to Vinnie. His loss was expected, after mobility became a huge challenge for him during his last year. Still, it was the most difficult thing I'd been through thus far in my life.

There is such a sanctity around taking care of an older animal. I'd never done that before, cared for an elderly animal… or elderly human either, for that matter. When Vinnie went through illnesses and challenges, I loved being there for him. It was difficult to watch him struggle, but caring for him was the best thing I could have been doing with my time.

I adopted him at 2 months old when he was younger than I was, I said goodbye to him when he was older than I was in dog years, and watching the entire arc of his life was one of the best gifts I've ever experienced.

Our last 24 hours together was perfect; I couldn't have planned a better last day for him. We went for a walk, I bought him Persian shish kabob and rice for his last meal, I gave him a big peanut butter treat, snow fell that night (or, as Vinnie and I called it, "free ice cream!"), and then we slept in until 10am the next morning. Vinnie and I loved doing that; he was the best sleeper-inner I've ever known. After we woke up, we headed outside to see his neighbor puppy friends. Then back inside for treats, lots of hugs and kisses, and then more treats. Then we waited for the veterinarian to arrive at our home. I held Vinnie's paw as he took his last breath, telling him I loved him and that he was a good boy.

I felt so alone after Vinnie died. My home, our home that he and I shared, was so quiet, empty, sad. I didn't want to be home, all alone with my grief, so I kept myself busy out and about as much as I could. Part of that was getting outside and going for long walks. And eventually encountering crows.

The crows became a consistent, daily presence in my life. They were amazing, funny, cute characters I could count on, some welcome interactions with other living beings when I didn't necessarily want to talk. And all the crows asked for in return were a few pieces of cat food and my company.

Crows are social animals (Black, 2013). Even when they are finished eating the snacks I bring, they still follow me just for the company, just like they did years ago when they joined Vinnie and me on our walks. There is something so heartwarming, especially after experiencing loss, about being greeted by 10,000 cawing, screeching crows every day who want nothing more than to spend a few minutes in my presence.

After Vinnie passed away, I spoke to an animal communicator, a medium, so that I could talk to my pup again. I had spoken to her once before he passed away, and found out all kinds of funny things that Vinnie was thinking about. Completely accurate facts about our life together, things that she would not have known unless Vinnie was telling her right at that moment.

"He's funny," the medium said. "He's got a great sense of humor."

Didn't I know it. Vinnie was always making me laugh; we spent our entire relationship playing games and having fun together.

As enlightening and beneficial as it was to talk to Vinnie through the medium while he was alive, I realized I needed to talk to him again after he passed away. One of the things that she said in our session was that Vinnie wanted to visit me in the form of a hawk.

"Oh... I walk with crows every day, and I think about him on my walks. Does he mean a crow?" I asked.

"No..." she replied. "He said he would come by and visit you as a hawk. So if you see a hawk, just know that it's Vinnie."

Well, I thought, I hardly ever saw hawks. Even walking with my crows for about 160 days in a row at that point, I had only seen a hawk a couple of times. I wondered why Vinnie would choose that as his vehicle.

But the next day, I saw a hawk. And then the same thing the next day, and the next. And then that weekend, when I drove down to Portland, Oregon for a couple days, I saw a hawk being chased by a few crows. Each time I saw a hawk, it brought tears to my eyes. If it really was Vinnie, he obviously made the effort to visit so many times right after he said he would. I really missed him, my goofy little pup.

Whenever I go for a walk now, I remember how the crow walks started: my pup by my side, our crows watching us from the trees. And whenever I see a hawk, I speak to Vinnie.

"Hi sweetheart! Remember to leave the crows, okay? Those are your friends."

And each time I say this, the hawk flies away and leaves the crows alone. Maybe it's a coincidence. Maybe the hawk doesn't like a human talking to him, interrupting his solo hunt.

Maybe it's Vinnie, remembering that he's in Woodinville to visit me and not to pester our crow friends.

"Good boy, Vin. See you tomorrow."

Vinnie's duck friends visiting us and literally standing on our boat!

I loved catching this wink on camera… some kind of secret code? Or an inside joke? "I know it's not a real hamburger, but thanks anyway, Mom!"

One of the many hawks I saw after Vinnie passed away.

Slurping water while drying off.

Crows watching me and waiting patiently for a snack…

…But sometimes being too excited to wait patiently, and instead creating pandemonium in the air!

Walking as Meditation, Walking as Healing

As I mentioned before, the long meditative walks started in early 2023. I walked so much that I was burning through walking shoes left and right (no pun intended), my walking mile time became 2-3 minutes faster, and I had a lot of time to think and meditate. It was such great therapy around grief, too, after losing my faithful 4-legged walking partner.

The river walks became my favorite. With each step, I recalled all the years of happy memories with my pup, years of laughing at Vinnie's silly antics, his mischievous glances at me as he climbed out of the river and shook off right by me. He loved to body slam me after getting all wet and muddy, which I pretended to be upset about as I fell over, laughing.

The first few months after his passing, I walked in a different city each day of the week. Edmonds, Bellevue, Seattle, Kirkland, Woodinville, Redmond. I even drove between 20-100 miles away from my home some days just for the variety, revisiting trails and rivers that Vinnie and I loved in Des Moines, Normandy Park, Burien, Bellingham, Mount Vernon, Sedro Woolley. I mention all these cities because if you know the Pacific Northwest, you know what a stretch it is between Bellingham and Des Moines, Washington. You may also be able to picture where I walked; each of these areas has beautiful places to hike and swim and have a picnic.

At one point during these first few months I wrote, "I'm not sure where I'm going on these walks, but I feel like I'm getting closer each day." Indeed, I think I was just trying to walk to the other side of my grief.

For whatever reason (maybe it was serendipitous), even though I'd been mixing it up and walking in a different city each day, in late Spring I spent a few days in a row walking in Woodinville. If I hadn't, I don't know if this book or my crow relationships would even exist. My routine was to start along the river trail and then wrap around the other side of the warehouses to complete a 4-mile loop. On the fourth day of consistent Woodinville walks, I tossed some crackers I'd been eating to a couple of crows that were lingering around the warehouses.

If you are familiar with the area, you may be familiar with the Pacific Northwest Crows. I am so grateful not only that I live in this area with thousands of crows, but also that they are studied and researched extensively. One of the most famous researchers of corvids is John Marzluff, a wildlife biologist and professor in Seattle (University of Washington, 2024). He has written books about crows and other corvids, and gives talks and presentations. I was grateful to be able to attend one of his presentations, and I also watched his TEDx talk about corvids. Check it out online, and listed in the References page (YouTube, 2014).

You may also know that the Woodinville area is home to approximately 10,000 crows during the day. At night, they roost in Bothell, Kenmore, Redmond, and other nearby cities, but during the day, there are thousands upon thousands of crows that hang out in Woodinville (University of Washington, 2021). There are a lot of different farms, fields, and wineries in Woodinville, and the crows love to look for seeds and dig through the grass for snacks.

At least, I think that's what they love about the area. They probably also love that it's a tourist town, and that there are tons of restaurants with outdoor seating (people leaving food and crumbs behind), and baseball and soccer fields that also draw a lot of crowds and families. Crows are not really forest birds, seeking privacy and darkness and seclusion, at least not during the day. They love the cities and towns and people.

On this fourth day in a row, I didn't think too much of my snack delivery. I love crows, but I think on this particular day, I was getting tired of carrying the crackers on my walk and I knew they'd love to eat them. The couple of crows gobbled up the crackers, and we went our separate ways. However, the next day as I was walking along that same spot, there they were again. But this time I didn't have snacks.

Whoosh!

Something brushed by my hat. It surprised me, but I wasn't scared. It only took a couple seconds for me to realize that it was a crow.

"Hi!" I called out to him. "Did you want a treat? I'm sorry! I don't have anything right now."

But that gesture, that assertive "greeting" by the crow, changed my life in such a positive, wonderful way.

"I'll go grab some snacks, okay? Wait here. I'll be right back."

I quickly walked to the gas station around the corner and bought some crackers, and then walked back to the place where I was greeted. Amazingly, they were still there. Waiting for me? Maybe they understood my tone of voice and the meaning behind my words, "Wait here." But how could they? Do crows really understand humans so well?

I opened the crackers and sprinkled a few of them on the ground. A crow, probably the one who had brushed by me, flew down and grabbed a piece. A few of his friends joined him and they all gobbled up the snacks.

"I'll see you tomorrow, okay?"

And then almost every day for the next year, I walked by that same spot and fed the crows. This single, isolated spot turned into 2 different spots, then 4, then dozens and dozens along my 4-mile loop. Actually, it's no longer different individual spots, but a constant stream of flying and skipping and swooping and sprinting crows, and I love it. I love when they find me along the trail, when they see me across the river and fly over, when they emit a surprised clicking noise and hop over to me. It is especially impressive when they find me out and about, because the times of day I walk are so inconsistent. But as I said, crows hang out in

Woodinville all day and keep their claws on the pulse of what's happening around town.

Those initial couple crows in late Spring 2023 turned into thousands of crow friends. My extroverted pup Vinnie would be so proud of me.

On many days of my early grief, the crows were the highlight of my day. They were a connection to the animal world, a brief escape from isolation and loneliness, and witnesses to my meditative walks without having an expectation of me to talk.

That is one of the many reasons I loved my life with Vinnie; I could be quiet or loud or happy or sad or contemplative, and he was fine with it all. He accepted me as I was, every single day. I feel that is how the crows treat me; sometimes I talk to them, sometimes I'm listening to an audiobook through my headphones and I just throw treats for them. Sometimes, when there is a downpour and I don't want to get completely drenched, I drive to some of the main rendezvous spots instead of walking. This has only happened a handful of times, and my crows don't mind; they see my car and fly over. They are fine with it all.

(•ᵥ•) (•ᵥ•) (•ᵥ•)

One day in December 2023, I found it difficult to get out of bed. I wanted to stay there all day, the covers pulled up over my head. We all have days like that, sometimes for reasons we can identify, sometimes not.

I love who I am, and I love my life. But life can knock us down, too. On this particular day, I just felt sad, like I was grieving 100 different losses all at once. In those last few days of the year, I was grieving all of the difficult events I'd gone through in 2023, a year that was probably the most challenging and heartbreaking of my life. But beyond my own life, I was feeling sad about world events, the Middle East, the upcoming election year, the state of the world, climate change. I was grieving tragedies in the news, and people's pain all around the world. It felt overwhelming, and I just wanted to stay inside and not do anything.

But then I remembered that anywhere from 1 to 10,000 crows would be waiting for me to show up for our daily walk. Or at least they'd be happy to see me if not exactly hanging around waiting; crows have busy lives! And I remembered that it was supposed to be sunny, a rare but welcome occurrence in December in the Seattle area. I had plans later that day with a friend to go to a holiday festival. And my friend has dogs I was excited to see. And, And, And.

Before I got out of bed, I checked Facebook. A post I had made earlier that week was simply, "Tell me something good," and I scrolled through my friends' beautiful responses. They were all so touching and wonderful, and they lifted me up. I decided to get out of bed.

I walked a fast 4 miles, the fastest I'd walked all year. My crows were wild and delightful, as always. They got super close yet were polite, doing spins and flips and making me laugh. A crow on the other side of the river saw me and flew over, circling over me 2 times and doing little loops as he kept his eyes on me the entire time. I tossed him some snacks, but he didn't want any. He had just wanted to say hello, and that touched my heart.

I felt so much love for them. They helped me get out of bed that day, and a few other times in the months since Vinnie had passed away.

My crows give me a daily task: trading snacks for the gift of being in the presence of animals. Their antics, acrobatics, and greetings, landing on the tree branches above my head, hopping over excitedly when they see me, the juveniles screaming in my face when they get excited about the snacks… I love it. And I love when they get closer and closer to me with each passing day, showing me they trust me.

The weight of the world is still heavy. But I can do more for the world if I'm out there loving people and dogs and crows than I can by staying in bed all day. I just need to remind myself of that every so often.

Walking is a healing activity, and it is also wonderful exercise. Low impact, easy on the joints, minimal chance of injury in relation to many other cardiovascular activities (Rabbitt, 2024).

Walking is great for emotional and mental wellness. Indeed, as I tell my therapy clients, moving is a great therapeutic technique, whether it's walking or swimming or jogging or yoga. It's a great way to settle our thoughts, invigorate our creativity, and produce those wonderful feel-good mood chemicals, dopamine and serotonin and endorphins.

Walking also helps to give us answers to things we are struggling with; research shows that throughout the beginning eons of humanity, our brains developed in such a way that movement enhanced our problem-solving abilities, our ability to think under pressure. When our ancestors hunted wild animals for survival or had to run to protect themselves from danger, they had to be quick thinkers (Rhodes, 2013). Because of this, our brains evolved to work the best while we are moving. This is one of my favorite theories about the human brain.

Test it out in your own life. For example, have you ever gone for a walk with a friend, and maybe you were talking about something serious? And by the end of the walk, you felt like the problem had been solved? Or maybe you at least had a different perspective on it?

And if you're not able to move as much because of mobility issues, time, or other constraints, there are studies that going for a drive also helps with solving problems. Getting out, maneuvering our vehicles, solving the maze of our roads (Lancaster University, 2016). Other repetitive motions and actions have a similar effect on people: knitting, washing dishes, putting together a puzzle, playing certain video games like Tetris or word games… they all help us think more clearly as we simultaneously work through challenges and problems (Butler, et al., 2020).

My preference has mostly been walking in nature because I enjoy getting away from the traffic and noise of the city. I love finding elements of the natural world, bunnies and crows and deer, herons and cranes and ducks, the river trail and the mountain path, the wooded forests and ocean walks. It feeds my soul, and when there are animals present, it's even better.

So, walking and thinking as I was processing grief and loss, reflecting on memories of Vinnie, laughing at the tricks and antics my crows were up to while also appreciating the connection we had with each other... all of these were incredibly healing for me.

The day before the 1-year anniversary of Vinnie's passing, I was walking on the bridge above the river by Willow's Lodge, a hotel and restaurant in Woodinville. On this day, the blue sky and fluffy white clouds were so beautiful over the water, and I stopped to take a picture.

At that moment, a crow landed on the bridge railing and looked over at me. When he saw what I was doing, he also looked out across the river.

"Are you checking out the view too?" I asked him.

When he looked at me again, I tossed him some treats. I continued past other famous Woodinville landmarks right there, the Herbfarm, The Barking Frog, and the cluster of wineries there at the Old Redhook Brewery.

A few feet further down the path, another crow landed on the wooden fence lining the trail. He suddenly lost his balance, distracted by looking at me, and his whole body swung forward before he caught himself with his claws that were tightly gripping the wooden fence. It was like he got so excited to see me that he didn't pay attention to where his feet had landed. It was adorable, and I started laughing.

"Hang on there, buddy. Here's some snacks. Don't get too excited to see me; it's the same stuff I brought yesterday."

I feel so grateful to have these crows in my life.

WORTHY CAWS

WORTHY CAWS

Different views each day…

Checking out the river view with me… Or just enjoying the chaos!

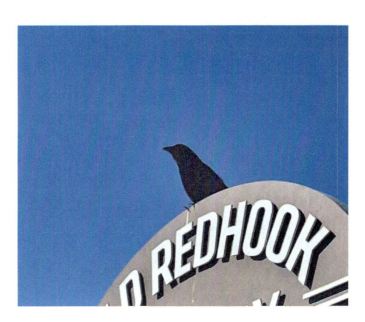

One of their favorite spots to wait for me as I walk down the trail.

This cute little guy was so fluffy… He landed, looked at me, and then shook off the rainwater from his feathers. I've also noticed that sometimes the crows "shake it out" and readjust their feathers and posture as they wait for me.

I love when they stretch their wings!

"Your order has arrived"

Sometimes I feel like a "Meals on Wheels" driver, or delivering the crows their DoorDash or GrubHub orders. When it's pouring down rain, I don't want to do the 4-mile walk. Even though I was born and raised in Seattle and have experienced many activities in the rain (soccer, running, camping…), it really wears on a person after several decades. After raising Vinnie and going on several walks every day and getting soaked 8 months a year, I need a break. So, sometimes I take the easy way out and provide meal delivery service for my crows.

For my fellow Seattleites that may be thinking I'm weak right about now, I'd like to clarify that a little rain is okay with me, if it's just sprinkling or misting. But on the downpour days, the days that soak through your pants and shoes in a matter of seconds, I will drive.

By the way, Seattleites have a dozen words for rain:

Sprinkle	Deluge	Pelting
Drizzle	Raining Cats and Dogs	Mist
Shower	Coming down	Flood
Downpour	Beating down	Storm

Sometimes we just say, "It's wet out there" or, "It's disgusting outside." These words and phrases describe different things, and we all know what each of them means.

As I drive, I focus on our previously-agreed-upon meeting spots to deliver food to my crows. Just like when I walk, this started out as one solitary spot, then evolved into 2, and somehow now traverses the entire 4 miles. Part of the 4-mile loop is inaccessible by car, but I can usually get to 5 or 6 of the main spots before the trail disappears into the park or other super secret paths.

When I'm walking, they recognize me right away, no matter what I'm wearing. But I soon discovered that my crows also recognize my vehicle, as they will fly right over as soon as they see it. This is great when I'm parking my car and about to start walking, but it's a little strange and awkward when I'm just going to the grocery store or the bank. More on that later.

On these driving delivery days, there is something so satisfying about being greeted as soon as I pull into the parking lot or swing by the field they're grazing in. Sometimes I get out of my car and they immediately start to call their friends over, and other times, I'll just toss the snacks out the window. And then it's pure chaos.

The first few times I tossed the treats out my window, they were too scared to come up to my car door. They stared at me through the car window, their beady little eyes silently willing me to drive off so they could grab the food. It reminded me of Vinnie, when I would grab the treat bag and take one out for him. As soon as he saw what was happening, he stopped whatever he was doing and stared at me with such intense concentration.

At first, I didn't realize the crows were waiting for me to drive off before partaking. On a few of these rainy days, I tossed out the snacks and waited in my car for a couple minutes before driving away. As soon as I started driving, I noticed the crows all flew in for the treats. I felt bad I made them wait, but this entire experience has been a learning process for all of us. And after a few times of this, they started feeling more comfortable and coming up right away before I had a chance to drive out of there.

"Your order has arrived," I say to them as I put the car in reverse. They're not great at tipping me, but it's okay.

On one particular afternoon, I threw some treats down and a crow wasn't paying attention. He was standing right in the center of my back-up camera, and I had to wait a few seconds for him to leave. I slowly started to back up, and my camera caught him in the frame, letting me know how far he was from my car.

Thankfully, he noticed the car inching towards him, and he finally hopped to the side.

One time, a crow didn't want to land where the other crows had congregated to grab some snacks, so he flew after my car as I approached the stop sign and railroad tracks. There were no other cars around, so I tossed a couple treats out my window. This guy reminded me of a dog chasing a car.

I try not to throw things out my window, but if I'm on an empty road or driving slowly through a neighborhood and I see a crow rooting around in the grass, I will roll down my window and whistle to them. When they look up, I'll toss out a little snack. They get so excited; it reminds me of a parade, where I'm throwing candy and the crows are like the kids scooping up the Starburst and Tootsie Rolls.

These crows have such a special place in my heart. I hardly ever drive past a crow, whether he's standing atop a telephone wire or rooting around in the grass in a neighborhood greenspace, without pulling over at the next available turn so I can talk to them. Even if I've just finished a 4-mile walk or doubled it for the 8-mile route, I will still stop on my way home if I see them. I keep snacks in the trunk of my car, so I am always prepared for these spontaneous meetings.

This doesn't just happen in my hometown with *my crows*, but wherever I am; out of town, in another state, etc. Any potential chance I get to interact with them is too tempting to forgo. It's not dissimilar to seeing a dog out in public; it's so difficult to resist asking the owner, "Can I pet your dog?" I can't help it; I truly love them.

WORTHY CAWS

The Start of the Crows

Alfred Hitchcock's movie, "The Birds," is powerful and terrifying. And when one watches this movie at 6 years old like I did, it stays with them forever.

When I was a kid, I spent tons of time at my grandparents' house. My brother and I were there almost every weekend and many evenings, the Christmas holiday break, Spring Break, and summer vacations. We went camping, we spent hours and hours outside climbing trees and building forts, we went to Duvall Books (a wonderful long-standing used bookstore that eventually closed in 2016) where our grandparents bought dozens of used books for both of us. My grandparents were both elementary school teachers and encouraged us to read and write as much and as often as we could.

And we watched movies. My grandpa loves movies of all decades, genres, and quality: silent black and white films, the Golden Age of Hollywood, Oscar-nominated films, 1980's B-movie cinema, and modern films made with CGI. He has a huge movie collection, thousands and thousands of VHS cassettes and DVDs.

One day, I decided to watch "The Birds." I was much too young to be watching such a movie, but I had read on the VHS that Suzanne Pleshette was in it, and I loved her. I had seen her in "The Bob Newhart Show" via Nick-at-Nite reruns, and in a Disney film with Dean Jones called, "The Ugly Dachshund." That funny kids' movie was about dogs, I reasoned, and "The Birds" must be about adorable little birds! I thought it was a perfect choice for a lazy Saturday afternoon.

My grandmother walked into the living room as the movie was wrapping up, and she immediately recognized what I had watched. She handled it so well; she sat down next to me and made lighthearted comments about the movie, talking about how crows weren't scary in real life, and that the movie was just an overdramatization. A comedy, if you think about it, she reasoned. Besides, Suzanne Pleshette had indeed survived the murder of crows (pun intended) because she was in *our* living room, on *our* television every night with Bob Newhart. She was practically *family*, wasn't she?

  These comments were all so beneficial to me, as they eliminated any feelings of fear I had. I also believe that it was this early exposure to the movie and her comical comments about crows that made me feel so comfortable around them throughout my entire life. Even now decades later, when I watch "The Birds," I can remember her funny, reassuring comments.

  Over the past year, many of my friends have asked me if I name the crows.

  "No," I reply. "There are thousands of crows in Woodinville. A few have distinct markings, but I don't recognize the majority of them."

  The only crow I ever named was a crow with a damaged wing. I saw her several times early on in my walks, and I named her "Suzanne." This crow was strong and resilient; she had a hole in her wing, but it didn't seem to bother her. She was still able to get around well and grab snacks, often the first one to arrive at the scene. She was beautiful.

  Because of "The Birds," I have always given such reverence to crows. When I was younger, I gave them space and tried not to bother them. We've never had any issues between us.

  This reverence is one of the reasons I wanted Vinnie to leave the birds alone. I didn't want to do anything to upset them, and I wanted the crows to feel safe with us, a human and a goofy weird-eared pup.

  I once had a friend who really loved Tippi Hedren. She loved her as an actress, and followed her career and personal life. She loved "The Birds," and other productions Tippi had been a part of, and also loved Hollywood in general. She and I bonded over this shared interest. My friend passed away a few years ago, and afterwards, the movie and Tippi and crows became more meaningful to me. It is because of my friend that I have a photo of Tippi on my living room wall, and a signed thank you card from her when I donated to her wild cat sanctuary. It makes me think of my friend and some of the conversations we'd had, and I feel so close to her with these wall decorations.

    Every day on my crow walk, I think of my grandparents, and my friend, and Tippi and Suzanne, and Vinnie. They all bring such joy to my heart.

A bit of chaos and pandemonium, but I've noticed that they hardly ever fight amongst each other for snacks. There seems to be a hierarchy, or maybe even just respect amongst themselves, about letting some grab the snacks while others watch and wait. Even in big groups, there isn't any scuffling. The only time I see scuffling is in smaller groups of 2 or 3. But this is extremely rare.

I love how some crows are demonstrative and theatrical here, and some are so casual and unfazed.

Lots of farmland, community gardens, lavender fields where the crows chill during the day before they return to a nearby town to roost for the night. One of my favorite spots is between the farms and Chateau Ste. Michelle Winery, north of Tahoma/Mt. Rainier.

My 10,000 friends with Tahoma/Rainier in the background.

Shenanigans

One of my favorite things about crows is their capacity for fun. They fly around all day, searching for food, getting into trouble with people and other birds and animals. They are highly intelligent, and I believe this leads to their propensity to seek out trouble.

    I also believe that my daily walk gives them an opportunity to get into more trouble. From that day when a crow brushed up against me to show me that he was there and was demanding food and attention, to the wild flight patterns they exhibit right in front of me, to the ways they interact with each other... I love their antics and shenanigans. And crows love shenanigans.

    And yet, like Vinnie, they also seem to be averse to shenanigans. Like Vinnie, who thought it was okay when he himself participated in mischief but didn't like it when others did, the crows seem to have the same opinion. They will call each other out, squawking and antagonizing each other, when they don't agree with other crows' behavior. Many different times, they have told their fellow crows that the food I've thrown down for the whole group is just for them, not to be shared. A few times, although rare, they have gotten into physical scuffles with each other over the snacks.

    "Hey!" I say. "I have more treats. There's no need for this gratuitous physical violence."

    At the sound of my voice, they separate, and then I throw down more snacks. They happily hop over.

    "See? Just chill out a bit. There's enough for everyone."

I'm not sure if I'm supposed to intervene with the animal kingdom like that, even just vocally, but how can I not? These crows are important to me; they're like my children, my pets, just like Vinnie was. When Vinnie was at the dog park and another dog would bother him, biting or pestering him, I would intervene. I had to keep him safe, and I want to keep my crows safe, too.

(•ᵥ•) (•ᵥ•) (•ᵥ•)

Crows are brilliant. They recognize faces, and will tell their family members and friends all about you, whether you've been kind to them or made them upset (Hamilton, 2012). This is a protective mechanism; crows need to be able to share vital information with others to protect their community, but to also let everyone know if you can be trusted and if you might have some food or other resources to share with them.

Professor Marzluff told a story in his TEDx talk (YouTube, 2014) about a guy who pretended to throw something at a corvid. After that, the birds pooped on the guy's side of the car, but left his wife alone. Switching sides with his wife to see what would happen, he found out that the birds switched sides, too… pooping only on his side, seeming to intentionally target it for his behavior towards them.

Crows remember. They are just trying to survive, like all of us. This story is kind of funny, but it also teaches a lesson: actions have consequences, and often it's better to just let nature co-exist with us as much as possible. Besides, crows are cute and clever and fun to watch.

(•ᵥ•) (•ᵥ•) (•ᵥ•)

Crows bring a sense of mischief to my life, something that has been missing since Vinnie has been gone. I love it when they zip right by my ear, or *whoosh* right over the top of my head.

Sometimes I will look straight up, and the tip of my baseball cap will almost brush their belly as they fly over my head. I believe they get super close to me on purpose, to play with me a bit, to see what their own limits are and what are mine. I have this image that they one-up each other to get as close as possible to me, either touching me like a few of them have, or just getting so close that the hairs on my skin move.

More than a few times, a crow has landed right next to me, on a sign, a fence post, or on the ground next to me. They look at me as soon as they land, and sometimes, when they are especially close, they look startled. The first time this happened, I imagined what the crow was thinking.

"My friends dared me to land this close! But it wasn't my idea, I promise!"

I reassure them that it's fine, that they have nothing to worry about, and then I toss them a treat. They are so cute and their daredevil antics make me smile every time.

A few months after I started walking with my crows, there was a week where I was pleasantly harassed by a rowdy group of what I assumed were teenage crows. All week, they flew super close to me, did fun and creative dives and spins in the air, and were noisy and boisterous as I fed them snacks.

One day I was getting prepared to go on my walk, and was at my car organizing my phone, wallet, and keys. Suddenly, there was this loud, insistent squawk behind me. I laughed, and then slowly turned around. The juvenile was a few feet away from me, so excited and impatient for treats. He was adorable.

"I'm so sorry that I'm not ready yet! Here you go. I'll see you later on down the trail too, okay?" I said as I tossed him a treat.

I read that the more vocal ones tend to be juveniles and teenagers, and that once they mature, they don't make nearly as much noise (Birdfact, 2022). This makes sense; they are asking their parents for food, they are developing their sounds and voices, and as they are growing into adulthood and maturing, they are figuring out the world around them. I love when they're noisy and wild, and I love when they're quiet and gentle. I love it all.

(•ᵥ•) (•ᵥ•) (•ᵥ•)

One day, I thought I'd ruined my relationship with my crows. I was giving them some Cheez-Its and pretzel mix. I always start with cat food, but if I run out, I have to run into a gas station or other business to grab some replenishments, and today's option was a bag of Cheez-Its and pretzels.

    Suddenly, 3 crows got into a physical scuffle over the handful of crackers and pretzels I'd thrown down. This was the first time I'd seen them argue with each other where it turned physical. I felt like I was at the dog park watching some pups jump on each other, and I quickly walked over to them, all piled up on the grass, all 3 screeching and yelling.

    "Hey!" I yelled, clapping my hands.

    It took them a few seconds to hear me, or to register that I was talking to them, but then they scattered. They all flew off, not just the 3 in the scuffle, but the whole group of about a dozen.

    As soon as they flew off, I was scared they would never come back. After all, it took 6 months for my crows to be okay with me turning back around and watching them while they were eating. (For the first few months, they would immediately fly away and scatter if I turned around to take a picture or to just watch, which is actually a great survival instinct they have. I'm not a hunter, but I would imagine it's common for hunters to scatter food on the ground to gather their target, and then attack.)

    After I yelled at them to separate and they all flew away, I threw down a few more handfuls of treats. A few of them returned, and this time there were no fights. As I walked away, I hoped they wouldn't tell their friends that I was yelling and clapping at them; I wasn't sure if they would forgive me. But, they did. They were back the next day, hyper and wild as ever, and I was so relieved. I didn't see any more fights for a couple of months after that.

(•ᵥ•) (•ᵥ•) (•ᵥ•)

Crows, especially juveniles, love to play. Not just with me, but with each other. Sometimes, I'll throw down a couple treats, and one crow dives for it while another crow dives for the first crow, cutting him off before he can grab the treats. The first crow will try again and again, and each time his friend will chase him away without having any care for the treats himself.

"I have more…" I call up to the second crow, and toss a couple treats a few feet away. But at this point, it's a game, and he is having a wonderful time teasing his friend.

One time, 2 crows were play-wrestling in the air right by my head. They were behind me, but I could hear loud noises, wings flapping together, not because they were in flight but because they were in a play-scuffle. The noise got closer and closer, until finally I saw them fly over my head, not more than 3 inches from the bill of my hat.

"Hey! That's enough. It's too much," I said, as if I were separating 2 children who were getting out of control. "You can fly by me, but when you're wrestling that close to me, it's too much."

They stopped wrestling, separated from each other, and then came back for some treats. I was happy about that, but then self-consciously, I wondered if other people on the trail had witnessed me having a conversation with crows. Oh well.

(•ᵥ•) (•ᵥ•) (•ᵥ•)

After a few months of our relationship, the crows started floating above me as I walked. I was *thrilled* with this new development in our relationship.

"What are you doing up there? Coasting? Are you a kite? You're so cute!"

It always looks like they are paragliding, just hanging out up there, peaceful, letting the wind carry them. We will make eye contact, me walking and them floating, and it is so surreal. Around the time this started, I decided to start tossing treats up in the air so they could see them better. I toss the treats directly in front of them, and then they swoop down and grab them from the grass. I'm waiting for them to catch them mid-air like dogs do, and I'll let everyone know if we develop a circus act with this.

(•ᵥ•) (•ᵥ•) (•ᵥ•)

One thing that alarmed me the first couple of times, but which now barely phases me, is when they fly extremely close to me if I don't feed them quickly enough. If I'm rummaging through my bag, that's okay because they seem to know that I'm grabbing the snacks. But if I continue walking forward to try to get to a better area or a clearing on the path (often to get on the other side of a person on the trail who is walking towards me so as not to scare the other person with my murder), sometimes the crows will almost fly into me. They will whiz by my ear, or almost brush my shoulder, or fly right by my ankles and land a couple feet in front of me, literally forcing me to stop in my tracks and feed them. I now love it when they get close, but it was intense the first several times. Now, our interactions feel so natural that I have to remind myself that they *are* wild animals.

One afternoon, they were so out of control that I wondered what was going on. I had missed my crow walk the day before, one of the only couple of days I missed all year, and I wondered if their excitement had been building up. Or maybe it's not all about me; maybe they were just having a hyper, frenetic day.

In any case, they were pushing each other off tree branches and flapping their wings wildly. At one point along the walk, we saw an eagle, and they all flew right above my head for half a mile like they were trying to protect me, or maybe thought I'd protect them? A few times, they chased each other mid–air as they flew right past my ear, like they wanted attention or were giving me an acrobatics show. One guy saw me across the river and flew over, and when I made eye contact with him, he suddenly got scared and returned to the other side. I stood there for a few seconds and called him back over until he returned.

At one point when I was on the river side, I was walking along and heard a gentle "caw." It sounded something like,

"Hello Ma'am, did you see us here?"

I turned around and there were 2 patient crows perched on a branch above me, waiting for me.

"Hi there!" I called up to them. "No, I didn't see you there! Thanks for cawing out."

I tossed them some treats and they flew down to scoop them up. I'm so glad they said something; I often have my headphones in, and sometimes I miss the fluttering of their wings nearby. When I'm not listening to anything, I can usually hear even the quietest crow flying near; my ears have become so attuned to them.

That same day, I noticed so many crows letting gravity take them down to the ground. I would toss some treats, and they would make eye contact with me as if to confirm, "Is that for me?" It reminded me of Vinnie, when I would grab a delicious treat for him and he would look at me as if to say, "Really? Am I dreaming?"

After these crows made eye contact with me, they would just freefall to the ground, daredevils who love risky tricks. Also, I love when the crows make eye contact with me. It makes our connection seem so personal, like we are just 2 beings communicating with each other.

Flight patterns

There was this great sketch comedy show from a few years ago that was filmed in Seattle. "Almost Live!" was televised on KING TV Channel 5 before Saturday Night Live every Saturday night, and it was all about Seattle inside jokes and personalities. One of my favorite skits was about a single afternoon in Seattle: after a long Winter, the clouds clear, the sun shines through the atmosphere, and the rainy city of Seattle finally comes alive. People strip down to their tank tops and sandals, and go sunbathe on a beach in West Seattle. A couple hours later, the rain returns, and in the skit, people put their clothes back on and go back indoors until the next sign of Summer (King TV, 2020).

    One day in March 2024, on one of the first genuinely sunny and warm days of the year, I thought back to that skit. Everyone got a little excited. Seattleites were swimming in bodies of water, people were walking around half-naked, and the whole region stopped hibernating to spend time outdoors. People were so excited for a glimpse of the upcoming Summer. I was one of them. I love Seattle Summers more than most things in the world. Needless to say, my walking trail was packed.

    Suddenly, a crow flew right over my head as I was on the other side of the river, and it was so loud that it made me think of the Seattle Blue Angels. The Blue Angels are the US Navy's flight squadron, and they do several air shows in Seattle every year.

"*Zooooom!*"

    The sound was so close that I was certain he was going to hit me. I laughed, and then gave him a treat. It was the loudest, zoomiest, fastest flight sound I had ever heard from a crow, and it was *awesome*. It was also slightly terrifying, in that way that you trust the rollercoaster operator that the ride is safe and that it's fun-scary, not scary-scary. I trusted this crow dude that he wasn't going to slam into the back of my head.

The crow gobbled up the treat, and then a few seconds later, I heard it again.

"Zooooom!"

This was entirely my own doing, as I gave him positive reinforcement after his first Blue Angels flight over me.

But I love when they get almost aggressive in their connections with me. Because I do trust them; they have never done anything that has hurt me or truly scared me.

A few times that same day, they flew right towards me, seemingly absent-mindedly but probably knowing exactly what they were doing. I wondered if they would notice where they were going before flying into my face. But then they made eye contact and averted their path a few inches so as to avoid collision. One time, I looked up and there was a crow right above my head. I threw down some treats for him, and he free-fell directly at me before adjusting course.

"Wow, that was so close!" I teased him. "You are all getting comfortable with me, huh?"

Their shenanigans really remind me so much of my life with Vinnie. I loved him for so many reasons, I loved everything about him, but I especially enjoyed his mischief. I know my crows are not puppies, but sometimes they really do feel like puppies.

WORTHY CAWS

A crow yelling at another for their shenanigans.

Looks like they made amends.

Skidding to a stop as his friend is yelling about something.

Ballerina moves, with an audience of one.

Lots going on in this picture!

Tell your crows I said hello

My family and friends, my community and connections… they are all the best. They are so supportive and encouraging of all my hobbies and activities and little quirks.

This includes my crow walks. As soon as I started posting stories and photos of the crows on social media, people started asking me about them.

"What do you feed them?"

"Do you walk every day?"

"Do the crows bring you gifts?"

I love talking about crows. Their habits, a funny story that just happened, some little incident where they SQUAWKED or sneezed or flew right by my ear. I try not to post about them every single day, but it's so difficult. I love them.

And then people just started saying,

"Tell your crows I said hello."

It always touches me to hear this. First, that people realize the love I have for the crows, and second, that my crows are like my pets. They're *my* crows, even though of course they don't belong to me. Not even Vinnie belonged to me; he was always his own person with his own identity and life. But they are mine in the sense that I care for them and love them, and check in on them every day.

People always asked about Vinnie too, sent him birthday cards, gave him Christmas gifts, and invited him to parties. They treated him like he was my son (he was… and still is), and they were emotionally invested in him.

I feel like my people are invested in my crows, too. For Christmas in 2023, about 6 months after I started my Crow Walks, my best buddy gave me a huge bag of peanuts. It was the perfect gift. I get emails and texts and Facebook messages, "How are your crows?" People send me cards with crows on them, and stickers, and memes and videos and Zoom events about everything crow-related. I love it.

And yes, deep down I know that they are interested in my crows because they're interested in me and they love me. I feel the love, and I'm so grateful.

One of my favorite photos I've ever taken. I hope he's noticing his shadow and how regal and beautiful he is.

I love these photos; the awareness the crows and I have of each other, the mutual trust and agreement to interact yet another day.

Before many close-up photos, I usually say, "Wait. Stay right there. I wanna take a picture." I said that to Vinnie, too. I'm glad they pose for me. And when I tell the crows, "You're so pretty," they often look down. How? Why? I don't know, but so, so cute.

A Sense of Humor

"What are you doing?" I ask, as 2 crows whiz by my right earlobe, so close that I wonder if they actually touched my skin or just the little hairs on my skin. But really, isn't that basically the same thing?

They sail a few feet above me, almost touching each other but in perfect harmony. They twist and turn through the air, their path looking like a DNA strand. It is chaotic but beautiful.

If the crows would let me, I'd pet them and hug them. I have such "cute aggression" (Participant, 2013) towards animals, dogs and birds and other animals. Such a dimorphous response that I experience every time I see something overwhelmingly cute.

The crows haven't allowed me to touch them, at least not yet anyway, and maybe they never will. But when they fly inches from me or crash into me, I think they do this to mess with me and to tease me. They must know that it could be somewhat alarming, even for me, to have thousands of crows swarming me, but they do it anyway. Maybe they sense that I want to touch them, and so they know they can crash into me and I don't mind.

My dog Vinnie did the same thing when we were at the park or the beach; he would stand 100 feet from me and then suddenly get this mischievous gleam in his eye. I would brace myself, knowing what was coming. And then he would run! He could sprint so fast, and that was one of his favorite things to do. He always had the biggest smile, and would run straight at me before swerving a couple inches to his left to avoid a collision. He was playing a game of chicken and teasing me, and I loved it.

Crows also show other signs of having a great sense of humor. Not only do they love flying right by my ears and over the top of my head, but they love doing half-circle flights around my legs. As I'm walking, they will circle around the outsides of my ankles and land in front of me, asking for treats in such an elegant, artistic way. As they fly and land and fly and land along my walk, it feels like they are laying out the red carpet for me… announcing my arrival to their friends all along the trail, a few steps at a time.

They love to play and chase each other through the air. They chirp and "caw," to me and to each other. They seem to get so excited and even hyper when I walk through our predetermined rendezvous spots. Maybe it's the draw of the treats and snacks, but because I've witnessed them ignore the treats and still fly with me, my presence alone seems to activate something within them. They act like a bunch of wild teenagers sometimes, vying for attention, showing off and making as much noise as they possibly can.

One day, I was on the phone with a friend while on my crow walk. This was early on in the crow relationship, maybe just 6 weeks or so, mid-Summer 2023.

"I love how they don't squawk at me anymore! They just silently fly up to me every night."

Before that sentence was out of my mouth, several extremely loud crows came squawking up behind me, staring straight at me and landing in the branches above the trees. It was as if they were waiting for that exact moment to prove me wrong.

"Never mind," I told my friend, laughing.

Before I spent 13 years of my life with Vinnie, I didn't realize that animals could have a sense of humor. Actually, I didn't know much about animals before Vinnie, despite having family pets growing up. But he showed me time and time again that not only did he find things funny and often hilarious, but he was able to participate in jokes and even initiate jokes and teasing on his own.

Why wouldn't animals have a sense of humor and appreciate jokes like humans do? Sometimes I think we (humans) think we are better than other species, and thus assume some things are exclusively just for us. Yes, we can drive cars and build smartphones and whatever other advanced skills we have… But given all the problems even just those 2 items cause, is it really "smarter" that we have incorporated those things into our lives? And we definitely don't have the monopoly on emotions, simple or complex. It reminds me of a quote by Jane Goodall:

"You cannot share your life in a meaningful way with a dog, a cat, a rabbit, a rat, a bird… and not know that they have emotions similar to ours" (Samuel, 2021).

I clearly saw these emotions of joy, happiness, humor, and an appreciation of fun in Vinnie, and I see them in my crows as well.

WORTHY CAWS

The Introvert's Dilemma

One day as Spring 2024 was gearing up into full swing, there was a crow who flew over to me and circled and circled over my head, trying to find a place to land. He finally found a spot, but it took a couple minutes because for a while, we were surrounded by flimsy little shrubs and blossoms that wouldn't hold his weight. The ground was covered in long blades of grass from the recent rainfall and Spring sunshine, preventing him from landing there as well. On any other day, he might've just landed on the trail by my feet, but there were hundreds of walkers and bikers on this rare Sunny Seattle April day.

"I don't know where to throw the treats," I told him. "The grass is too long and you'll never find them."

I threw some cat food anyway, and the kibble immediately disappeared in a green sea of blades of grass.

The crow kept flying East to me, then back West across the river, back and forth a few times. Then we reached a clearing and I called him over.

"Here, let's try here," I called, pointing to a spot.

He immediately saw me pointing from hundreds of meters away, followed where my finger was directing him to, and landed on a little dirt path between the blades of grass. I threw him some treats.

We were so in sync, he and I, having the same mission of getting him snacks. It was magical.

I love my crows, but I'm private about interacting with them in public. I'm such a painful introvert, comfortable around friends but embarrassed to be having long corvid conversations in the middle of a group of strangers. People on the trail were watching this entire exchange, and I just pretended they weren't there. I know I'm the Weird Woodinville Witch Woman and that's okay, but I'm acutely aware that murders of crows follow me all around town and the attention they, we, attract. It doesn't only feel magical, but I'm sure it looks like magic too; I call them over and they fly over, landing inches from me. I use different sounds, whistles and kissing sounds to communicate different things. I speak their language and they've got me totally trained.

Vinnie drew me out of my *Introvert Comfort Zone of Safety* too. We'd be going for a walk, and he wanted to talk to everyone, walk over to them and wait for them to pet him, which they always did because his Weird Ear and goofy smile were so welcoming. People would come over and ask if they could pet him, photograph him, hug him. We were at an Everett Aquasox "Bark in the Park" baseball game once and he walked over to a whole other family sitting on the lawn. He plunked down, looked over at the gentleman he'd chosen to sit next to, and smiled, tongue hanging out the side of his mouth.

"Are you okay with him there?" I asked.

"Yeah, we love him!" they answered.

He hung out with them for 20 minutes, just sitting there watching the game and letting the man pet him, before returning to me. He was so good with everyone and everything.

I, on the other hand, was perfectly fine going through life never meeting my neighbors. I was content walking on the trail or going to the park with just Vinnie, or maybe Vinnie and a close friend or 2. But he never let me get away with that. We always had to *interact* and *socialize* with everyone within a 5-mile radius, and it was exhausting. But it was probably also good for me. He, Extreme Extrovert Labrador Retriever, was the opposite of me, and sometimes we need those opposite forces in our lives to help us grow and learn and progress.

This is especially true after the pandemic, which made me even more introverted than I originally was. Vinnie helped me do that, and now the crows are helping me too. We live in community for a reason, and maybe it's okay that the good people of Woodinville witness my crow conversations. I won't stop walking or talking with my crows, in any case.

Gifts

Crows have been known to bring people gifts in exchange for the snacks and food that we give them. This makes sense within the context of crow behavior because crows are transactional beings. Order, consistency, routine, predictability.

I didn't think this would ever happen to me because I feed the crows out in the community instead of at my house. The crows probably don't know where I live. Also, I'm unpredictable in terms of timing: I don't have a set schedule for when I walk the loop, do the double 8-mile set, or do DoorDash Delivery. It depends on the day of the week, my work schedule, any non-crow plans I have (yes, I do have human friends and non-crow plans sometimes, FYI), the weather, and the time of the sunset based on what part of the year we are in.

However, one day shortly after my crow walks started, I saw a crow feather on my doorstep. I picked it up and walked out into the clearing where my car was parked.

"Did you guys leave me a feather?" I asked into the wide-open sky, just in case they were in the trees above me, watching. "Well, thank you. I appreciate it."

One day on my walk, I found a man's wallet. I looked inside and saw a Chase Bank card, $13, a Driver's License, and some other random plastic cards. I dropped the wallet off at the bank later that day. I didn't think anything of it, until a few weeks later when I saw a turquoise and gold-plated bracelet on my walking trail.

The place where I found the bracelet, just like where I found the wallet, was on a super secret hidden trail where no one walks but me, as far as I can tell. It's secluded, isolated, and where the gravel rocks are so big that it's not the easiest trail to walk on unless you have sturdy hiking boots.

At first I thought, "Oh no! Somebody lost their bracelet."

Since I was in the middle of the wilderness away from where people would be walking, I just left it there. But the next day, it was still there.

Now thinking that maybe a crow left it for me, I picked it up. The crows had seen me walk this same exact trail for about 315 days in a row at this point, and maybe they put it right in the path of my feet so I would find it.

Suddenly, I had a horrible thought. What if the wallet with all the cash and credit cards a couple months prior was something a crow had stolen? And then dropped it in my path as some sort of payment for the treats I'd given them?

A couple days after I found the bracelet, there were some Velcro straps in my path. Still in a plastic package, unused.

The thought of crows stealing jewelry and wallets to then give to me makes me laugh, but I also feel bad for the original owners. I hope they don't steal anything else to give to me.

The R-Rated Movie

When I was 16 years old and a Junior in High School, my friends and I went to the movies on a Friday night. I don't remember which movie came out on that particular Friday, but the cinema was packed and the ticket lines stretched into the parking lot.

Whatever movie we wanted to see, it was R-Rated. We thought we could get in; who checks IDs for movies, anyway?

Well, the woman at the ticket counter checked our IDs. And I was just a few weeks from my 17th birthday, but that wasn't close enough to get by. My friends were also 16, a few months younger than I was.

After we were rejected at the ticket counter, we turned and walked dejectedly away.

"Well," I said. "What should we do now? Is there anything else you want to see?"

Before my friends could answer, a young man walked over to us. He looked barely older than us at maybe 21 or 22.

"Hey," he whispered. "Come with me."

I looked up at him. He had on a black baseball cap, a black t-shirt, and khaki shorts. I looked over at my friends, looking for answers. What did this guy want with us? But they smiled back at me, and then I understood. I handed him the $15 or whatever it was for 3 movie tickets back in 1999, and he turned back around and ordered our tickets from the same woman who had rejected our attempt just seconds earlier.

"Thank you!" I said as he handed me the tickets.

"Shhh... No problem," he whispered. And then he was gone.

Sometimes my crow interactions at age 41 remind me of that ticket-buying experience at 16.

I recently went into a store in my town to grab some things, a store I visit less than once a year. When I came back out and started walking to my car, I heard a familiar but surprised sound.

"Caw?"

I looked up and saw one of my crow friends sitting atop a light post in the middle of the parking lot. We must have been friends, because he clearly recognized me... but had never seen me in this location before.

"Hi buddy!" I said. "Did you want a snack?"

And then I looked around surreptitiously, peering out from under my black baseball cap. No one was nearby, but we were still in the middle of the parking lot, surrounded by cars and potential onlookers. What to do?

I still, after almost a year, feel self-conscious and shy about feeding my crows in public. It's not illegal to feed birds (otherwise we wouldn't be able to buy birdseed or hummingbird feeders anywhere, right?), but it makes me nervous, especially when my murders follow me all over Woodinville. We seem to have our own secret private witchcraft language of chirps, whistles, and hand signals, even though half the time I don't know what I'm doing.

"Hey, come with me," I whispered to him much like the 21-year-old whispered to me decades ago. To make sure the crow got my meaning, I also used one of our secret hand signals.

We rendezvoused over by the fence along the outer edge of the company's property, and I gave him a few peanuts. He hopped excitedly, ate a couple, and took the others home with him.

The next day, I returned one of the items I had purchased. It wasn't the right style or size, and as I left the store with my revised receipt in hand, I saw my crow friend fly up to the same light post he'd been sitting on yesterday. Wordlessly; this time, no squawk or caw or even little chirp from him. I followed suit and didn't say anything.

Crows and humans are such creatures of habit, but it was still serendipitous that he saw me. On this second chance meeting, it was a few hours later in the day than the time I'd visited the store the day before.

I peered up at him again, leaning my head back to see past the bill of my black baseball cap. Wordlessly, I opened my trunk, grabbed a few cat food pieces, tossed them under the light post, and climbed into my car. As I pulled out of the stop, I unrolled my window and tossed a couple more for him. He excitedly hopped over. Clandestine snack witchcraft handshake deal complete.

So many of the interactions with my crows are like that. Secretive, quiet, under the radar. Sneaking them snacks and hoping I'm not upsetting or offending anyone by doing so. I guess if that's the most mischief I get into, I'm doing better than when I was 16 and my friends and I were sneaking into R-Rated movies.

WORTHY CAWS

More favorite photos…

Sometimes they fly over but avoid eye contact (left), and other times look at me intensely (right).

Wiping raindrops off his nose, onto the bench!

Wet and disheveled, yelling at the rain (or maybe at his friend).

Chateau Ste. Michelle Winery

A rainforest, or Woodinville?

WORTHY CAWS

A crow defying the rules.

A heron, ducks, and crows all having fun at the park.

Goofing Off

Just like my pup used to do, sometimes my crow friends are just goofing off.

When Vinnie and I went on walks, he would meander and dawdle. He was a Labrador Beagle mix, 2 breeds known for having an amazing sense of smell used for hunting, sniffing out drugs, detecting various illnesses, etc. Vinnie loved to sniff everything: grass, flowers, bushes, plants, cute little bunnies... But it always took such a long time. He could spend 5 minutes checking out a single blade of grass.

"Hey, quit goofing off. Quit screwing around," I would call out, teasing him in a silly singsong voice. "Let's go, Vin!"

He would smile, his big, ridiculous smile, and trot along after me. Until the next interesting blade of grass caught his attention.

My crows fly towards me and towards the treats, becoming more and more brave about how close they get to me. As they fly, they goof off so much. Sometimes they tangle with their buddies, caw at each other, chase each other. They look to their left, to their right, above and below, basically every direction but straight, as they fly straight at me.

"Quit goofing around!" I joke to them. "Watch where you're going so you don't fly into my face."

They look at me then, and quickly avert their route so they don't hit me. Crows are great at responding when I speak to them.

Sometimes, instead of making a judgment on whether they're goofing off or not, I'll simply greet them.

"Hey buddy. Do you see me here?"

Again, they will make eye contact with me. I probably don't give them enough credit. Crows probably know exactly where I am at all times; they find me all over Woodinville, after all. But it's still somewhat alarming when they're speeding towards me while looking at their buddy to their left.

However, on one afternoon, I don't think the crow knew where he was going. I was at the park, and he flew right by my chin, just outside of the frame of my sunglasses. A combination of his position, and my vision being obstructed by my sunglasses frame, I didn't see him until the last second. I thought he was going to fly into my face.

"Aaaaaccck!" I said out loud.

I looked over to my left, and he had landed and was standing there in the grass. He looked just as scared as I had been.

"I'm sorry. I didn't mean to yell at you," I said. "I thought you were going to hit me. Are you okay, buddy?"

He looked at me, and I tossed some treats down to him. He hopped over and gobbled them up.

"I'll see you tomorrow," I said.

Sometimes I throw treats for them when they are looking somewhere else. The snacks just sit on the ground, unnoticed.

"Are you guys even paying attention? Don't waste it," I call to them. "Unless you want to find me some more wallets to fund your snacks."

A crow's best sense is their vision (Nichols, 2023). If they don't see me throw the treats, they are not likely to sniff them out.

Whenever they don't seem to notice, I will walk over to where the treats are and look up at my crows.

"Okay, do you see me? Are you paying attention now?"

I'll throw another handful down, on top of the original pile.

"Did you see it?"

Most of the time, they fly or coast down at the second serving. But sometimes they're not interested in snacks; they just want company.

"Well now you're just wasting it," I say. "Are we just goofing off today?"

I laugh and continue on my way, and they fly after me, doing their ridiculous acrobatics and flips, competing for attention.

WORTHY CAWS

More snacks!

As I've described in an earlier chapter, this whole crow relationship inadvertently started because I had brought a couple crackers with me on a walk one day. Once I realized they wanted snacks and expected them after that first day, I started bringing stuff with me every day. Peanuts, trail mix (all chocolate removed beforehand), cat food, popcorn, dried fruit, dry cereal, chips, and sometimes crackers and crunchy pretzels. I only feed them crackers sparingly as I've read that bread and gluten are not the best for them (Andrei, 2023). About 99% of the time, I feed them cat food, as it's easy to buy in huge quantities for reasonable prices (thank you, Target, for your 16-pound bags for less than $16).

However, once word got out that Katie had the snacks, more and more crows started showing up. Hundreds, maybe even thousands some days. And in those beginning days when I was trying to gauge how much I'd need, and fit everything into the pockets of my gym shorts during the summer months of shorts weather, sometimes I ran out of food.

On one hot day in July, just a few weeks into my crow walks, I had given out all of my food about halfway through my walk. I'd only brought a single bag of treats because I hadn't seen many crows the last few days. It had been so hot that entire week, and the crows had been sparse.

Crows wear black suits and black leggings, and the heat seems to affect them more than it does me, in my summer attire of a light-colored tank top and shorts. It is not uncommon to see them standing on a phone wire or in the grass and just panting, their cute little beaks open. But usually during hot weather, they're nowhere to be found, hopefully staying in the shade somewhere. Maybe they're all poolside at a rooftop rager.

In the second half of my walk on this scorching summer day, a crow flew over to me.

"Hi, buddy," I said. "I don't have any snacks left. I gave them all away."

He looked at me, and as I continued walking, he followed me.

"See?" I said as I took the empty snack bag out of my pocket and turned it inside out. "It's all gone."

I walked over to the big green dumpster and threw the wrapper away, and looked at him as I did so.

"All gone."

I felt exactly like I always felt when talking to Vinnie when I had to assure him that we'd eaten all the food.
But the crow kept following me. First 100 yards, then 200, then 400.

"Did you just want to hang out, or are you hungry?"

He kept following. Not squawking or invading my space, but just following me, landing on the building gutters and tree branches above my head.

"Okay. Stay here, and I'll go get you something. Okay?" I reassured him.

I walked to the gas station and quickly grabbed some trail mix. I backtracked to where I was before, and the crow and one of his buddies flew up to me, landing in the trees above.

"Hi! Here you go!" I said as I threw the snacks on the ground. "You owe me $3, okay?"

Since I had backtracked anyway and it was still so hot and light outside, I decided to do the reverse path. A 4-mile day turned into an 8-mile day. Have I mentioned how much I love Seattle Summer?

I've probably had to run into the gas station a couple dozen times in the past year of my walks. I always try to overestimate how many crows I will see, but sometimes I gauge it wrong. Or sometimes the crows tell so many of their friends, and a small little get-together turns into an out-of-control frat house party. A couple of times, the crows will "walk me" over to the gas station and wait outside while I replenish the snacks. One time, I was grabbing the treats and heading to the cash register when I looked out the glass door and saw the crow waiting for me, standing on the "Welcome Mat" right outside. It was adorable. He knew he couldn't join me inside the store, but he was waiting so patiently right outside.

(•ᵥ•) (•ᵥ•) (•ᵥ•)

One of the most ridiculous, extravagant things I have ever done for my crows happened near the beginning of our relationship in the Summer of 2023. I hadn't been feeding or walking with them for too long, and so on this particular day, I had forgotten to bring snacks with me. Now, I carry several huge bags of cat food in my trunk so that I never run out, and fill little Tupperware containers that I then throw into my backpack. But back then when I was younger and more naïve, I would bring snacks from home every day. On this Summer day, it slipped my mind.

I started walking and was about a mile in when I realized I didn't have any snacks in my pockets. I considered going back to my car, but I knew I didn't have anything there either, and so I'd have to drive to a grocery store or the gas station to get something. And what if my crows saw me on the way back to my car, and I didn't have anything to offer them? I wasn't scared of them, I didn't think they'd attack me, but as we were building up this new relationship, I didn't want to disappoint them after they'd started to expect treats.

As I thought about what to do, I realized there were a few dozen wineries between where I was standing right then, and where the crows and I rendezvous each night. I walked into the nearest winery. I had been in this winery before, and it was expensive, but as I walked in, I hoped maybe they had some cheap crackers or something.

I reached the host stand and looked at the menu. No crackers. But it looked like they sold charcuterie boards to accompany wine tastings and happy hour. Maybe that would work. I quickly glanced at everything else on the menu, and realized the charcuterie board was probably going to be the easiest thing to split up and share with my crows.

It was also the cheapest item on the menu, but still pretty expensive. I ordered and paid, and with tax and tip, it was a whopping $25.

"I can't believe I'm doing this," I said under my breath. "A $25 charcuterie board for birds that know how to dig out of the dumpster."

I should put a money jar somewhere hidden along my walk, I thought, and they can drop coins into it to help support this snack habit they have. What's money to them? Maybe that's why they lifted a wallet for me a few months later.

But also, who am I kidding? These crows are my beloved pets. I would do anything for them.

I continued on my walk, charcuterie board in hand, and soon a few crows flew over. There was a picnic table nearby, so I walked over there and unwrapped everything, and the crows and I shared a picnic together. I gave them the items I knew they could eat, dried fruit and nuts, and I ate everything else.

It must have looked funny, but I love my crows so much. If you're ever in Woodinville and you see a grown woman having a picnic with a bunch of crows, just keep driving and never mention it to anyone.

(•ᵥ•) (•ᵥ•) (•ᵥ•)

Crows will verbally ask for snacks. Not just the loud squawking and cawing they do when they zip over to me, but in other ways as well.

One time, I ran out of snacks a couple blocks from the gas station. I rounded the corner by the old Woodinville sign by the now-defunct railroad, and saw some crows waiting for me. One crow greeted me with the cutest, gentlest little sound, like a little "hello." He was happy to see me but was quiet and shy about it. I emptied the last couple crumbs onto the ground in front of them.

"I'm all out, but I will go get some more," I told them.

About 10 crows followed me to the gas station, and I quickly got in and got out. As soon as I emerged, I opened up the bag of snacks, but there was a guy sitting in his car right outside. I didn't want to feed my crows in front of him or cause any sort of disturbance, so I kept walking down the sidewalk a bit, creating some distance.

When the crows saw me walking away from them, they made the cutest little sounds. It sounded kind of sad, like,

"Where are you going? Did you forget about us?"

I stopped in my tracks right there and sprinkled some snacks on the sidewalk. I didn't want the crows to ever think I was ignoring them or leaving them without a word. Crows have feelings too. As soon as the treats hit the sidewalk, they flew down and grabbed them. From that moment on, I tried to remember to always tell them what I was doing, just like how I spoke to Vinnie in complete sentences. Sometimes it does seem like they can read my mind, but if they don't react to a glance or when I point somewhere, I make sure to verbalize it to them.

"Let's go over here, okay?" I will now say, pointing to a grassy spot or a little further down the road, away from people, dogs, or cars. "Here you go, buddy."

They are so smart; they follow me and watch closely to where we can conduct our business. Because snacks are important business.

One day, I cleaned out my cupboards, grabbing anything that I thought they would like but that was slightly expired. Cashews I hadn't gotten around to eating, crackers, dried fruit. I took the entire lot with me on my crow walk later that afternoon, and went through bag after bag.

They loved the guava crackers, the cashews, and the raw almonds. But when I threw the dried apples and pears, one crow picked up a piece in his mouth, and immediately spit it out.

"YUCK!" he seemed to say.

I laughed. Luckily, I had a handful of almonds left, and I tossed those to him. He quickly gobbled them up. I'm not sure why he didn't like the dried fruit, but I'm glad I could give him something else to cleanse his palate.

One weekend afternoon, maybe reminiscing about the charcuterie picnic we shared months earlier, I wanted to share a meal with my crows. They're social, I'm sometimes social, we both like food, and I wanted to eat together.

Rusty Pelican is a great brunch place in Woodinville. It's usually packed, especially on the weekends. But it's easier to get food more quickly if you order carryout. Perfect for another picnic with my crows.

I ordered some waffles and potatoes and picked them up. Then I drove back to the warehouse side of my walking loop, an isolated place where I get to interact with my crows quite a bit without a human audience. I pulled into a parking space and waited. Within a few seconds, a few crows showed up, recognizing my car. I unrolled the window and tossed out some potatoes. I also had some other snacks in my car, cashews, pecans, and some Cheez-Its.

They loved it, all of it. One crow fit 4 Cheez-Its in his mouth, with a little shuffling and a few attempts. He somehow stuffed all of them into his mouth in a nice and tidy little stack, slanted a bit like when dominoes knock each other down. I got a video of the whole thing that I later posted on Facebook. I was laughing so much; it was adorable.

I ate my waffle, and then tossed out the last ¼ for the crows. I assumed they would tear it up into pieces as I had seen them do with other snacks, but a single crow grabbed it. The waffle was almost too heavy for him to lift up for takeoff. The other crows around him looked disappointed that he took the entire thing, so I got out of my car and grabbed some cat food from my trunk, and poured it onto the beauty bark for them. They were so excited, not seeming bothered that this was the consolation prize.

The crows always stuff their mouths as full as they can. They will try to stuff 3 peanuts into their mouth, although I've only ever seen them successful with 2. They will stack the peanuts on top of each other, horizontally, and in their beaks it looks like they are wearing those false Halloween teeth that kids buy as a part of their costumes. I wonder if the crows have any idea how ridiculous and adorable they look.

One day, after giving a crow some cat food kibble, he flew up to the top of a light post and looked down at me, asking me for more. I could see his throat was already full. They seem to store the smaller snacks in their throat and neck area as they fly off, either to share with their buddies and children, or to save for later to eat or to hide somewhere.

"Did you get some?" I asked. "Do you want some more?"

He looked at me and swallowed once, twice, three, four times until he ate all the food and his throat returned to a normal size. I laughed.

"Here you go," I said as I tossed a few more snacks. Maybe he could save this second batch for his kids.

(•ᵥ•) (•ᵥ•) (•ᵥ•)

Sometimes I will see my crows wiping their nose on a tree branch. I'm not sure if this is because they inhaled some of the cat food kibble powder and their nose itches, or if they are cleaning their mouth, or what. It usually happens after I feed them and they are coming back for seconds, or if they're seeing me for the first time that day and wipe their beak in preparation for snacks.

One day, I gave a solitary crow a bite of my sandwich, and with that little bite he also got a bit of cream cheese. As he gobbled the bread, he left a spot of cream cheese on his beak.

"Oh, you've got something on your beak... right there on the... Goodness you're so cute."

I wanted to reach over to him and help him wipe his face. But he must have felt that something was there because a second later, he walked over to some blades of grass and used them like a napkin, cleaning his beak.

One other thing I love is when they grab a few snacks, and then fly off a few feet to go hide the snacks in the grass.

"Oh, good job! Go hide it for later," I tease them.

Because honestly, they're surrounded by thousands of their crow friends and other animals in Woodinville, including rabbits, coyotes, deer, and other birds. Are they really trying to hide something for later? It doesn't seem too stealth.

The crow will fly to his intended hiding spot, and look back and forth from side to side to see if anyone is behind him, watching. He will look startled when he sees me behind him, and then seem to say to himself, "Oh, it's just Katie," and continue with the hiding of the treats. He will tuck the treat into the grass, and then look around for something to cover it with. Sometimes it will be a clump of grass from a lawnmower, or some small twigs. Sometimes, and this is my favorite because it seems the most ridiculous, the crow will grab a leaf and place it over the cat food.

"There. Perfect! No one will find that!" they seem to say as they take one last look at the leaf before flying off.

I wonder if they realize the leaf will blow away easily. But maybe they know something I don't about hiding snacks. In any case, it is incredibly cute.

Even more ridiculous was one day when I was giving them peanuts. I saw a crow place a peanut on top of the gravel trail, then look around for a few seconds before grabbing a pinecone, and then place the pinecone on top of the peanut shell to hide it. Really? Three odd shapes, gravel and peanuts and pinecones, all stacked on top of each other? I laughed at the ineffectiveness of that, but who am I to judge their hiding methods?

I love when they fly within inches of me, ensuring I see them, with the treats sticking out of their mouths… Almost like they're saying, "See? I got the snacks! Thank you!"

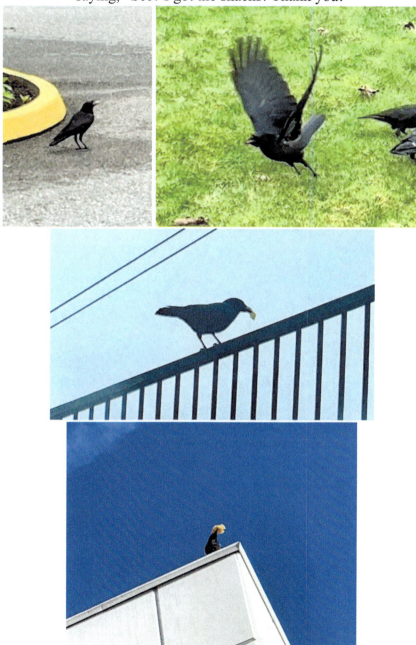

Hiding snacks in the grass, only to cover with a little leaf, tuft of grass, or pinecone.

Looking at me with snacks in his mouth.

Above: Foggy morning with a mouthful of treats.
　　　Below: Showing me the snacks as they're flying off.

Conversations with Crows

Crows pay attention to my voice, to what I say to them, as well as to what they can see. When I greet them and call out to them, they almost always make eye contact with me. Eye contact from animals can indicate a number of things, including a way to communicate and signs of intelligence (Heitanen, 2018). I also believe that it is a sign of a strong interpersonal connection with humans. The same thing occurs with dogs; they make eye contact with us as a way to understand us and to communicate with us, and when they're feeling calm and relaxed.

When crows are nervous, they look away. Maybe they've inadvertently flown too close to me, and are feeling timid and scared. Maybe we hadn't met each other yet, and at this first encounter, they hadn't yet developed trust with me. But once we develop trust and they know me, they make a lot of eye contact.

There is something so amazing about having a crow land on a tree branch a foot above my head and stare straight into my eyes, into my soul. It is magical. And as I mentioned before, I also love it when they're flying alongside me as I'm walking, floating to keep pace with my strides, and they look over at me from the corner of their eye.

"Yep, we're buddies, just traversing this trail together," I'll say to them.

When they stop near me, in the branches, on a fencepost or railing, on top of a street sign, on the grass, or somewhere along the pathway, I start up a conversation with them.

"You're so pretty. Can I take a picture?"

They wait there patiently as I take a photo, and then I give them some treats in exchange. When I tell them they are pretty, they often look down; like they're suddenly shy, or checking themselves out to see how they look.

As I'm walking and I see them flying towards me, I'll usually say something like, "Hey there! How are you?" I will make a little kissing sound at them, or whistle a few times. They know what I look like, but I wonder if they know the sound of my voice and the sounds of these little vocalizations too, if they associate them with me. They must.

As I wrote about in an earlier chapter, there are many stories about crows bringing gifts to the people who feed them. I'm not sure if I've actually received gifts from crows or if the wallet, bracelet, and Velcro straps were objects dropped by people. But the crows seem to thank me in other ways. They fly right by me, eye to eye, after I've fed them. They also make little cooing sounds, clicks, rattles, squeaks. Sometimes I'll throw some snacks, and they will make the most adorable sounds, like an excited gurgling. It sounds like, "Yes! She's got the goods!" The first time I heard it, I got worried because it was such a strange new sound that I hadn't heard before. I quickly turned around.

"Are you okay?" I asked, thinking he was choking on something I'd given him.

And then I just saw that he was really excited about the Cheez-Its.

"Be careful, okay? I'll give you the Heimlich if I need to, but please just be careful."

Crows have a similar brain composition to humans. They are self-aware, are able to recognize themselves in a mirror as opposed to thinking it is another bird in the reflection (Berman, 2020). They are as smart as gorillas, and like to be around humans, not just for the abundance of food but for the community aspects of living amongst humans. As I mentioned before in previous chapters, many times the crows would accompany Vinnie and me on walks even when they didn't want the snacks, and the same thing happens now when the crows follow me all around Woodinville.

I love how, after a few months, I started to hear different variances in their communication with me. It used to just be the typical "Caw, Caw." Now it's squawking, grunts, and sneezes, as their trust with me grows. It's like I've been let into the inner circle of communication.

One of my favorite things ever about my time with crows is when they emit a sound, maybe a "Thank you!" to me while flying by, their mouth stuffed with whatever snacks I've given them. A specific memory stands out, when one day a crow came over to me after I fed him, and I could see that his throat was extended a bit with the amount of cat kibble he had picked up. But still, he came over to land by me, and so I tossed a few more pieces. He responded by doing this little contented, satisfied, excited gurgle, except he had so much cat food in his mouth that it came out in this muffled sound.

"You're welcome!" I laughed.

I thought he was going to drop some of it. He reminded me of a kid with a bunch of candy in his mouth who is then given even more candy.

I also love when they stand over me, or fly by with the food sticking out of their mouth, as seen in the pictures above. On the rare occasion that I give them pretzels or popcorn, they will make a point to fly right in front of me (or even right by my car window if I'm driving away), the treats sticking out of their mouth. If you've never seen a crow with a pretzel sticking out of his mouth like it's the best cigar he's ever had… It's adorable.

I didn't know how much crows loved peanuts, but they go WILD over them. It is a magical thing to see, especially that first time when I didn't know what to expect. And in the style of them thanking me with other treats, after I gave them the peanuts, 3 crows all in a row flew in front of me, 1 by 1, each with a peanut sticking out of their mouth. It was the cutest synchronized "Thank you" ever.

Only one time did I ever see a crow who didn't seem to know what to do with a peanut. He quickly grabbed it up off the cement where I'd thrown it, and then dropped it from his mouth once, twice, five times. Was he expecting the shell to break?

"Have you never had a peanut before? It's not going to break by dropping it 3 inches…" I said to him as I watched, hoping he would figure it out.

He took it into the shrubs and hid it, and then returned to grab the second one I'd thrown him. I always tried to give each crow 2 peanuts, probably just because I like how cute they look when they stack both in their mouth like Halloween teeth.
For the second peanut, he immediately started pecking his beak against the shell, breaking into it.

"Ah, so you *do* know how to eat peanuts! What was going on with that first one?"

The only thing I can think of is that he knew I also had cat food, and wanted to trick me into thinking he didn't know how to open the shells? Are crows that clever? Even as I say that, I know that they are.
Once, I gave the crows some leftover chips I had in my car. One crow swooped down and grabbed 7 chips in his mouth. I couldn't believe how many he crammed in there.

"Good job, buddy!" I said. "Enjoy!"

I kept walking, and he immediately flew up onto the roof right above me, and looked down at me, as if to say, "Thanks!" The pile of chips in his mouth was almost larger than he was, and is one of my favorite crow photos I've ever taken.

One day, I accidentally snuck up on a couple of different crows. The first time, I was tossing snacks for a group of them, and when I turned around, one was right by my feet.

"Oh! I didn't see you!" I said.

He quickly jumped out of the way. I'm so glad I didn't step on him.

And then a few minutes later, I was by the Railroad Woodinville sign, right before The Cut Shop. I was walking through the grass, and suddenly, I saw a crow sitting there under a bush, just hanging out on the grass.

"Oh! I'm so sorry. Are you okay?"

But surprisingly, he wasn't scared and he barely moved out of my way. He looked fine, just content, like he was used to me and was one of my friends. I threw him some treats which he happily gobbled.

(•ᵥ•) (•ᵥ•) (•ᵥ•)

A hilarious moment happened about 6 months into my crow walks. As usual, I was ending my walk on the East side of the river, which is the opposite side of where I usually fed them for those first few months. Suddenly I heard a sound.

"SQUAWK!"

It was one solitary squawk, loud enough for me to hear it across the river. It sounded like a hello, like an acknowledgment that we were friends and he was saying, in *Friends'* Joey Tribbiani style, "How *you* doin'?" I looked over to the West side and saw 4 crows sitting atop a couple of trees.

"Do you want some snacks?" I asked them.

They didn't move, just remained perched on top of the 2 trees.

"I'll see you tomorrow, okay?" I told them.

And then, a few minutes later, I heard another squawk. I looked behind me and the 4 crows were flying towards me. They must have changed their minds about coming over. Even though I'm sure I had seen these same crows half an hour earlier when I was on the West side, I was so happy to see them again! I was thrilled that our connection had developed into a relationship where we were calling back and forth to each other across the river, communicating real information like, "Hello!" and, "Do you want snacks?" and, "Come on over!"

They landed in a tree above my head.

"Hey there! I have a few treats left, but that's it..."

I rummaged through my bag and threw down the last remaining snacks, 7 pieces of cat food. But they didn't want any; they just wanted to say hello to me and come visit me, which I absolutely loved. A few minutes later, they flew back over to the other side of the river.

(•ᵥ•) (•ᵥ•) (•ᵥ•)

One day I was standing by a sign in Wilmot Gateway Park, and a few crows flew over.

"Do you want a treat?" I asked them.

One sneezed in response, and it made me so happy. It reminded me of when Vinnie sneezed as a response to things, when he wanted treats or was trying to communicate something else to me. And I have to keep reminding myself that crows aren't puppies, because there are so many similarities. They scratch behind their ears with their feet, another thing that is so incredibly canine-like. Another thing that reminds me of Vinnie is when the crows shake off when it's raining. They gather all their strength and shake for a few seconds, feathers and fur becoming all ruffled and disheveled. And then the crows seem to take a deep breath, and every feather falls back into place. It is adorable, and I am so glad I walk during the rainy days too so that I can see things like this.

$$(•_v•) \quad (•_v•) \quad (•_v•)$$

On one walk, I lost my glasses. I usually bring my sunglasses when it's sunny, and put my regular glasses in my pocket or loop it through the neck of my shirt. This time, I put it in the same pocket as the treats, and they must have fallen out as I was taking the treats out.

The next day, I had my spare pair with me. I took them off and waved them around in the air above my head.

"Hey guys, can you please find something that looks like this, and bring it back to me? I lost my glasses yesterday."

They looked at me. I'm not sure if they had any idea what I was asking them to do, but I must have looked ridiculous that day on my walk, waving a pair of glasses a dozen different times in the air, yelling at the crows in the trees. I hope no one saw me.

They didn't return my glasses, at least not as of the publication of this book, but maybe they found them and brought them back to their roost. If they can find a use for them, then that's fine, too. I get all my glasses online at Zenni Optical for $6.95 a pair, so I'm happy to let the crows have a spare pair. At those prices, if you lose a pair on a crow walk and your crows aren't paying attention to where you dropped them, no big deal.

$$(•_v•) \quad (•_v•) \quad (•_v•)$$

"Got Snacks?"

One day stands out to me from one of my walks in March 2024. I think of it as the "Got Snacks?" day, although every day with my crows is a "Got Snacks" day if you think about it.

That day as I was walking, a crow called over to me from way across the river. Maybe he'd missed the food delivery when I was on that side, or he was still hungry. I'm not a crow, but his greeting sounded more like a question than Joey Tribbiani:

"Do you still have some snacks?"

They've seen me run out of food before on my walks, and I don't blame him for asking before flying all the way over.

I looked in front of me and saw a woman walking her dog, a cute and beautiful Golden Retriever. I try not to cause a huge disruption when there are people and dogs around, but it was just one crow asking if he should come over… I stepped over to the far left, off to the side of the trail, well out of the path of the woman and her pup.

"Come on over," I reassured the crow.

He immediately flew over, circling above my head and then landing on the grass next to me. I tossed him some snacks and then gave him some space to eat in peace.

As I returned to the trail, the Golden Retriever was looking at me with so much awe and respect. It made me laugh. I admit, I was too embarrassed to make eye contact with the woman, however. I do wonder what people think, Woodinville residents, both humans and dogs and whoever else may be observing this daily circus. I must seem so weird to them. But somehow these crows and I have learned each other's language, and we seem to know how to communicate.

Murder Me

"Murder Me" was going to be the title of this book, a play on words with respect to the collective noun of a group of crows. I thought that my desire that a "murder of crows" fly over to me would be well communicated with this phrase, like the slang, "Beer me" that was popular years ago. But, not everyone knows that "murder" is the collective noun, which then makes the title pretty dark.

My compromise is the naming of this chapter, all about calling and willing crows to fly towards me… much like I do with dogs, when I see them walking down the road or in someone's house.

"Come over here! Let me pet you, let me love you."

Calling them over often works with both crows and dogs, although I will admit that I've yet to pet a crow. It's okay; I'm perfectly content with our relationship as it stands now.

Whenever I see crows flying over or around me, I call to them. If it's near dusk and they are heading back home to roost, they don't visit. But if they are just cruising around, looking for snacks and company, more likely than not they will swoop down to my level. Especially if they recognize me. I can usually tell when a crow recognizes me, and likewise, I can tell when it's his first time seeing me. If he recognizes me, he will immediately come over, no hesitation, looking straight at me, a casual flight that sometimes gets super close.

If it's our first meeting, he will pause, look at me out of the corner of his eye, hesitate, hop around on the branch a bit, look away, and then come over while keeping a safe distance. I silently toss some treats and then continue walking, not making eye contact on this first visit, not wanting to scare them. This will usually be enough to reassure them that I'm safe.

I love feeding them, as the charcuterie picnic demonstrates. But I really love when they visit me just to socialize. I don't mind if they're using me for snacks, but it's heartwarming to know that sometimes they just want company, or want to observe me, or whatever else it is they're doing.

"You got nothing better to do? Do you want to walk with me for a while?"

And sometimes they will land on the trail, the paved path or the grass or the gravel, and walk ahead of me or behind me. I love this so much; they're cute when they walk, but I also love that we are just 2 beings, taking a stroll together on a lazy afternoon.

$(•_v•) \quad (•_v•) \quad (•_v•)$

I have learned that crows love consistency. They love patterns, they seek out reliability because they are reliable themselves, and they love schedules.

For example, one day I had to take my car to the mechanic and leave it there overnight. I decided to just walk home instead of call an Uber or a friend. Because of the location of the mechanic, I walked my path counterclockwise that day. The crows initially seemed really surprised and caught off-guard.

"It's still just me," I told them.

But because I also love consistency and I'm a creature of habit, it did feel a little strange to me, too.

I walk at different times throughout the day, but if I get there too close to dusk, I risk missing out on them completely.

On one Winter day in December, I arrived kind of late because a friend and I went out to lunch. And because it was Winter, the sun was going to set around 4pm. I quickly went to the park right after lunch, and saw all the crows flying above me to their nesting spot.

I was bummed that I missed them, but as I started walking back to my car, I told myself that there's always tomorrow. I looked up one last time, called to them and waved to them, but they didn't stop.

Suddenly, I saw a lone crow above me. He started circling, and swooped down in a dramatic, comical way. I laughed, but I was so happy and relieved that I got at least one interaction with a buddy. After his dramatics, he landed in a tree just a few feet away from me.

"Hi!" I called. "Did you want a snack for the road? Are you hungry?"

He looked over at me. He must have seen me walking down here as he was flying home, and he must have been one of my established connections, not a brand-new crow. I felt incredibly honored that he had decided to come visit.

"I'm going to take a picture," I said, taking out my phone and snapping a few photos.

They always wait so patiently when I take photos of them. I hurried so that I could feed him quickly and he could rejoin his group. He ate some of the cat food that I sprinkled around for him, and then took off again with his buddies.

"Thank you," I said to him as he lifted off. "See you tomorrow."

(•ᵥ•) (•ᵥ•) (•ᵥ•)

Sometimes the murder gets overwhelming. As I mentioned, this whole thing started with a crow or two. It has developed into organized chaos, which I love, but sometimes even I feel overwhelmed.

About 7 or 8 months after I started walking with my crows, hundreds started coming over to me by Willows Lodge. I sometimes park there in the trail parking lot by the baseball fields, and it is not uncommon that crows will come over and land on the fence railing before I even have a chance to park. I love that; the "Welcoming Committee." But as I start walking West, towards Willows and Chateau Ste Michelle, oftentimes hundreds of crows will see me from the fields to the south and come screeching over.

I am acutely aware that this is a walking and biking path, not to mention right along one of the main roads in Woodinville. Being both a people-pleaser and a corvid-pleaser, this 200-yard stretch is the worst part of the 4-mile loop for me. I don't feed them when there are people, dogs, bikes, and even cars driving by, as I don't want to create an accident or distraction. But as soon as there is a clearing, I give them some snacks.

And then watch out. Hundreds upon hundreds. Sometimes I just cross the street to the south, to the new "EasTrail" towards Tahoma/Rainier, where there are hardly any people and the crow commotion is hidden by trees and brush. It is these times when I most feel like I am in Hitchcock's movie, the difference being that my crows are incredibly polite and respectful of my personal space.

Sometimes I will call to them and they won't come over. In these moments, I wonder if these particular crows have never seen me before and they're unsure why this strange woman is yelling over to them. But because I've now yelled at them, I want to show them that I'm okay, that I'm a friend. At this point, I'll approach them and throw some snacks, and then we are usually instantly best friends.

Sometimes my murder comes over stealthily, silently. About half the time, I will hear a faint rustling of wings and feathers, and I will turn around to see some of my buddies in the branches above me. But sometimes I will just get a "feeling" that they are there, and I will turn around to find some friends silently waiting for me to notice them. I love it when they are loud and screechy, and I love it when they are calm and quiet. And if I don't notice them silently waiting, sometimes they will emit the cutest little greeting to tell me to turn around.

Sometimes they land in the grass and wait for me to toss them some treats. I don't throw the cat food directly at them, but a foot or 2 to either side of them so as not to scare them. Also, if it's a new crow who seems timid around me, I won't say anything so I don't intimidate them. Until we know each other, I'm just a silent crow-treat-dispenser. If we are friends already, I may joke around with them a bit and use a teasing tone.

"Are ya ready? Are you going to catch it? We have to get our circus act up and running."

A few times, I've thought they would catch the treats, but we haven't gotten that far yet.

In recent months, as I've mentioned before, the crows routinely fly East across the river when they see me. One time, a crow was making circles and circles above me and I was getting dizzy. I kept looking up, spinning around to follow his path, watching as he kept looking down at me and the surrounding ground for a place to land.

"What are you going to do?" I asked him. "Where are you going to land?"

He flew back and forth 6 or 7 times, until finally I got too dizzy. The next time, as soon as he was above me, I threw down some treats on the trail, directly in front of me. He immediately stopped circling and flew down for the treats.

"Phew! I was wondering when that was going to end," I said.

I felt so proud of myself because I felt like I was training him. Training him to stop circling, to just come down to the trail and have some treats. But then I realized that he was training me to throw the treats already, after his seventh roundtrip East and West.

"Throw the treats already, lady. Quit screwing around."

WORTHY CAWS

I love seeing crows waiting for me, one crow or a whole crow row!

Scratching behind his ear, he looked like a puppy!

Walking… in freezing temps, rain, and Seattle hoodie weather. (Photo on bottom right by Marisa Flores.)

Visitors

Many people have reached out to me and asked to join me on my crow walks. Maybe they've seen my social media posts and crow pictures, or I've talked about my crows with them. It is so fun when I get to bring a friend.

The first few times, the crows were a bit shy with a second person. But then they became more comfortable with the possibility of guests, and now seem to trust the other person right away even if it's that particular friend's first time walking with me.

I love the solitude of my walks, but I also love sharing my love and connections to crows with my friends. I even brought a puppy with me once, a foster dog I was taking care of from the nearby Homeward Pet Adoption Center. The pup did great; she was intrigued by the crows, fascinated even, but didn't seem scared. She tried to eat some of the cat food the first couple times I tossed it down, but then seemed to understand, just like Vinnie, when I said that was the crows' snacks. I distracted her with some dog treats, which helped.

One day, I brought a close friend with me. It was freezing outside, 12 degrees, rare for the Seattle area that rarely drops below 30 degrees even at the height of Winter. I asked her if she wanted to join me anyway.

"Do you go out in all weather?" she asked.

"Yes, unless it's a total downpour. But today is sunny, just freezing. And besides, *someone* has to feed them."

She laughed at the ridiculousness of this statement.

"Actually, they don't…" she reasoned. "Crows eat stuff out of the dumpster, the fields, parking lots…"

We laughed. Even though I know crows have survived for thousands of years without me, I feel so invested now. I want to make sure they are okay. Especially in those colder months, when the ground was frozen and people weren't having picnics or eating outside and inadvertently leaving little leftovers for them.
Despite the freezing weather, she agreed to join me. I wasn't sure what to expect, as this was her second walk with me, and we barely saw any crows on our first walk together.

"They usually don't come around when I have a second person with me, so I'm not sure if we will see any," I warned her ahead of time.

Sometimes I worry people will be disappointed when they join me on a crow walk and we don't see any crows, because they've seen so many pictures I've taken and posted on social media. They see these amazing, wild photos of crows flying straight at me and getting really close to me. I don't want to let them down.
But I shouldn't have been worried. The crows flew close by, did some tricks and spins, and generally didn't seem to be scared at all around her. She is also great with animals, and I should have known they would have been happy to see her too.
My sister-in-law also joined me on a walk. I gave her the same warning as I gave my friend, but again, no issues. As I hypothesized above, maybe once the crows realized I sometimes bring friends with me, they trust *everyone* I bring.
One day, a friend met me in the parking lot where I usually start and end my walks. She wasn't joining me, but I was giving her something for her dog, and the parking lot is a great central meeting point. I pulled in next to her car and we both got out of our vehicles. As we started to talk, I heard a loud sound behind me.

"CAW! CAW!"

I started laughing before I even turned around, and saw one of my crow friends standing on the gravel just a few feet behind me. I imagined him saying, "I see you've arrived. Where are the snacks?"

"Wow!" my friend said. "Do they always get so close to you?"

"Yeah… he probably recognized my car and flew over," I replied.

And then I addressed the crow.

"Just a second. I'll be right with you."

And because for the most part the crows are polite with me, he waited patiently. I finished my conversation and then threw him a snack. When I started my walk a few seconds later, there was a line of crows on the railing, waiting for me.

It's so endearing when they wait for me. Or when they meet me at my car before my walk, wanting to get a head start on a snack. I toss them a few treats before I start my trek, and they follow me sometimes to grab a few more.

(•ᵥ•) (•ᵥ•) (•ᵥ•)

Sometimes we have non-human visitors on our walk. I've talked about the hawks that hang out silently in the trees. There have also been eagles soaring above that the crows dive-bomb, out of protection or fear or shenanigans.

One day, I was about to feed a couple of crows who were staring down at me from a rooftop. Suddenly, I saw an eagle soaring several hundred feet away from them, behind them in the clouds.

"I'll give you some snacks, but you know there's an eagle behind you, right? Do you need to do something about that?"

They didn't do anything, but then I saw another crow chasing the eagle. He didn't call for reinforcements or anything, so maybe he was on "Eagle Duty" and these 2 near me were on a work break. As they stood there silently, waiting for me, I could imagine what they were thinking:

"Yeah, yeah, it's fine. Just give us the snacks, lady."

In addition to eagles, and thousands upon thousands of crows, Woodinville is home to large families of geese. "Gaggles of geese" to use their collective noun. Usually, I try to steer clear of them, giving them a wide berth whether I'm at the park or on the trail or anywhere else. They are sometimes so quiet (and like to hide in the grass too, just like crows), that I have accidentally walked up to within a few feet of them before one of them will stand up and squawk at me.

"Oh! Sorry, I didn't even see you there," I say as I back away and change course.

A couple of times, the lead protector goose will chase after me for a few steps before he gives up. It's always slightly terrifying.

However, one afternoon I went to one of the pre-established rendezvous that the crows and I had. I saw a few crows there and started to get out my snacks, but then I saw a family of at least 20 geese gathered there as well. They were about 50 yards away when I arrived, but the entire goose family walked over quickly when they saw me. This time, instead of the typical intimidating, scary posture they usually had when warning me to stay away, they looked earnest and gentle, like they were asking for something.

"What are you guys doing?" I greeted them. "Did you want some snacks?"

I tossed them some cat food, and soon had all the geese gathered around me. The crows weren't battling the geese for the treats; they were just looking at them respectfully, eyeing their size and numbers.

After a couple minutes, I decided it was time to continue on my walk.

"See you later, geese. Nice chatting with you. Hey crows, let's go over here…"

I pointed north, and the murder followed me to the other side of the parking lot where I fed them and resumed my walk.

It made me happy to have that moment with the geese, something that had not happened before or since. It also reminded me of a funny memory of Vinnie and I on the boat. I had been feeding the ducklings as the mother duck watched on, and suddenly the father duck showed up.

"I guess you can have some too…" I said, as I tossed the father some treats.

"Yeah, he used to be a baby duck too at one point," my friend said compassionately.

Suddenly, Vinnie stood right in front of me, blocking the treat distribution. He smiled and looked up at me, clearly wanting in on the treat action.

"Did you used to be a baby duck too?" I asked him as I gave him some treats.

There's enough to go around for everyone.

WORTHY CAWS

Some of our favorite rendezvous spots,
as dictated by the crows.

The neighborhood (crow) bar where we meet up…

He's showing me his graffiti art behind the crow bar.

10,000 Bodyguards

There's a scene in "Home Alone 2: Lost in New York" where the unhoused woman, played by the wonderful Brenda Fricker, feeds her pigeons. The viewer can tell that she and the pigeons have a special relationship, that there's mutual respect and trust between them.

When Joe Pesci and Daniel Stern, playing 2 criminals who broke out of prison, are chasing young Macaulay Culkin in Central Park, Brenda's character suddenly throws bird food on top of the 2 men so that they leave Macaulay alone. The pigeons dive-bomb Joe and Daniel, and Macaulay is safe, at least until his parents discover he's spent thousands of dollars on room service at the hotel.

I always thought the pigeon scene was really clever, but only while watching it during this past holiday season did I relate it to my crows in Woodinville. They have followed me around Woodinville for years and years now, with Vinnie and now by myself, and they are my buddies. I'm sure if I were ever in trouble, they would come to my defense, like the pigeons did for Macaulay. In fact, I read an article about how crows might even protect you. If you have a lot of crow friends, and they see you in trouble, there has been studied evidence that they will come to your aid (Insano, 2023). Maybe they have positive feelings towards those of us who are kind to them, those who feed them and talk to them. Maybe we are something positive in their lives, and they want to show us appreciation. Maybe they feel protective of humans, like dogs do. Maybe, like Vinnie, they just don't like it when others participate in shenanigans, and they are there to keep order over their kingdom. Because in some ways, doesn't it seem like the crows are in charge of things? Rough and tough, digging through trash, ubiquitous. Feared by many, loved by many. They rule the world.

I never feel like I'm in danger in Woodinville, a place I lived for 11 years. Vinnie and I used to walk at all hours of the day and night, sometimes taking a walk at 2am when we weren't tired, or when the hot summer heat had accumulated in our top-floor condo and we needed some cooler air.

Now, I live a couple miles from Woodinville, in a neighboring city. But I have so much emotional investment around Woodinville. It is down the road from Snohomish, where I was born and raised, and I have fond high school memories of driving down Highway 9 to go to the brand-new movie theater here, and then having dinner at Red Robin afterwards. Woodinville will always feel like home.

And even though I feel safe here, I do feel that the crows watch over me, and I love that. Sometimes they'll see me in different parts of town, away from our regular 4-mile loop, and they seem so excited to see me. I try not to feed them much outside of our loop, because I need to keep some boundaries on my time and the financial investment I put into this. If I had millions of dollars, I would spend all day walking dogs and feeding crows, but there has to be some limits. However, I will toss them a few kibble and say, "See you tomorrow at our regular spot." And if they don't recognize me, I will still toss them a few snacks, because they're crows and I'm a softie and a pushover... And then they will hop over and call to their friends, so excited.

$$(•_v•) \ (•_v•) \ (•_v•)$$

It took almost an entire year, but finally people around Woodinville have started commenting on my crow connection. For the first 10 months, there was only one instance when someone noticed, as far as I could determine.

On this day, a woman and I passed on the sidewalk near the old railroad tracks. There were a dozen crows behind me, all standing on the railing by the sidewalk, as I had just placed handfuls of cat food up there. The woman wasn't there when I did this, but suddenly she appeared out of nowhere. I was about to apologize, as she was going to walk right past my line of crows, but then I saw her smile as soon as she saw them. She looked surprised, like she didn't know what was going on, but she seemed to be getting a kick out of it regardless.

And then after those first 10 months, more and more people started noticing. They looked at me, initiated conversations and questions, and chuckled to themselves.

One day, a couple people commented on my 10,000 bodyguards. I was walking on the trail by the river, and a man a woman were walking their dog behind me.

"Do you walk this trail often? They seem to know you," the woman said.

She had just witnessed 4 crows seeing me from the West side and screeching over here to the East side before stopping right in front of me.

"Yeah, for almost a year. Sometimes they get out of control," I replied.

"They are really smart," she said.

A few minutes later, another woman with a dog saw me by Willows.

"Are you feeding them cat food?"

"Yeah," I replied.

"They are having fun," she said.

I agreed. The dog looked up at me and smiled, looking like he wanted to have some fun with us, with cat food and crows. He was a yellow lab just like Vinnie.

One day, I was walking back by the industrial area. No crows, no other humans, just a bunch of empty cement buildings. As I kept walking, 2 women appeared, going on a lunchtime walk.

Now, I know I'm not exactly "stealth," walking around a small town with a beautiful black cloud of 10,000 crows hovering above me, but during this quiet stretch, the 2 women walkers yelled over to me.

"Where are your birds? Where are your birds?"

"They'll be around," I replied.

I'd seen these women maybe 3 times over the past year, and they already knew I had a bird following? Apparently I'm gaining a reputation around town.
One day I went to a grocery store in town, and when I emerged, a crow greeted me in the trees right outside the door.

"CAW! CAW!" he bellowed.

"Wow! There you are," I said to him. "Come walk with me and I'll give you a treat."

He followed me to my car and I tossed him a few kibble. It reminded me of the time a few months earlier when I'd stopped at the store to grab a sandwich before my walk, and ate it outside at one of the picnic tables. A crow landed on the table next to mine and made heavy, intense eye contact. I hadn't been on my walk yet that day, and I felt guilty that I was eating lunch before feeding them.

"I'll be over there in a few minutes, okay? Here's a little snack to tide you over," I said, leaving a part of my sandwich crust for him as I walked to my car.

No wonder people in Woodinville have started to notice.

2,000 Photographs

So many photos. For this book, I sorted through 2,000 crow photos to find the best ones. To get to those photos, I had to scan 36,000 photos I'd taken since my first crow walk. The same thing happened when I sorted through literally 100,000 Vinnie photos last year to publish *Vinnie and his Weird Ear*. I take a ridiculous amount of photos, and sorting through them takes so much longer than the actual book writing.

A friend told me, "Next time, put them in folders."

A great idea, but I didn't know I was going to write a book about my pup 13 years later, and I definitely didn't know this crow thing was going to be a… thing. Life is interesting.

On my walk on a beautiful day in mid-Spring, almost a year into my crow walks, I was looking up at the amazing trees around me and just enjoying a rare 71-degree Seattle day. A couple crows flew over to me, 2 black shapes against the pale blue sky.

"I created this," I thought to myself.

It was such a strange thought to have, and as I walked I tried to figure out why it came to me. Finally, I determined that it was about the aspects of this situation in which I have control: the situation of living here in a Seattle suburb, a farm town that hosts thousands of crows every day that root through the fields. Arranging my free time so I can walk with them. Making sure I bring snacks that they like. Talking with them and learning how to communicate.

We do have a lot of control in our lives, either through overt actions, or manifesting what we want, or how we respond and adapt to things we have less control over. I also do have to give the crows some credit. And, I couldn't control where I was born, some past life events, the timing of circumstances, or parts of my identity where I have privilege.

But seeing 2 crows careen towards me at that moment, spotting me from across the river, I was so happy that I had done something in the past year that brought them over. My crows bring me so much joy.

One saving grace from spending so much time sorting photos is that each one brings back a memory, evokes some great emotion. I loved reliving my 13-year relationship with Vinnie when I wrote his book, and all the crow photos are such a delight to rediscover as well.

I Met Them at the Bar, and then We Played Hide & Seek

One day as I was walking, I put some cat food on the railing past Mercury Coffee. This is not a hand railing that people use to hold on to, but just a safety railing to prevent people from climbing down to the river.

I leave little piles of kibble here often, because it seems more dignified than throwing their snacks on the ground or grass. The ground is often full of puddles and mud, and sometimes the grass is so long that they can't see the treats. Crows deserve respect and dignity too.

On this particular day, I realized that placing food on the railing was like meeting them at the "bar." They wait for me on the telephone wires above, and as I walk past the railing, I leave 5 or 6 little piles of cat food, or peanuts, or cashews, for them to eat. They line up on the bar, and sometimes I turn around and take a cute picture of them all in a row.

Later, on the riverside trail, a couple of them were "cawing" to me across the river. I called them over and they were flying low near me, and I tossed the treats up in the air to see if they would catch it. They didn't, but one did a sort of halt and spin in the air as soon as he saw me throw them. It was so impressive, so acrobatic.

Then, a different crow "cawed" to me and I couldn't see him.

"Where are you?" I asked.

Usually when I ask this, they will shift their position a bit to show me where they are, either by jumping to a different branch, or moving a bit so the branch they're on shakes a bit. (Have I mentioned how smart they are?) Or they will fly towards me, probably thinking, "She is not that smart; I better just fly over there if I want any snacks." But this time, I asked a few times and didn't hear or see anything. I kept walking.

He "cawed" again. I turned around and there he was, 100 meters away, and flying towards me! I tossed some treats for him, but before he grabbed them, he flew away again.

"Hey! Where are you going? Are you taking off?"

And then I couldn't see him. He "cawed" again.

"Are you playing hide and seek?" I suddenly got it.

He emerged again and flew over with his buddy, eating the treats.

"I didn't realize we were playing a game!" I laughed.

I think this is intentional. Crows are brilliant; they also use their eyesight more than any other sense to navigate life (Nichols, 2023). It seems to me that if they are hiding, if we aren't able to make eye contact, they must know I can't see them. They also love to play games and tease others, as I've mentioned before. These games delight me, and they make my walks interesting. Something about me seems to interest them as well, as they certainly spend a lot of their time hanging out and playing games with me.

What a funny, wonderful relationship we have.

Love is Never Wasted

Love is so important, the most important and essential thing on this earth, I believe. And, love is never wasted. Towards people, or animals, or love towards anything really. Additionally, whether the love is returned or not, it cannot be wasted.

Sometimes I feel so ridiculous, leaving my house in 12-degree weather to feed crows that can obviously fend for themselves. As I've mentioned before, I always justify it to myself, saying, "Well, *someone* has to feed them." As if it's some sort of sacrifice, knowing fully well that I get more out of this arrangement than the crows do.

But I'm committed now. They helped me through grief and loss. They gave me a reason to get out of bed every single day and hit the pavement. I meditated, I listened to podcasts, I wrote my 2023 NaNoWriMo book via voice-to-text (not *Worthy Caws* but another book I probably won't publish). That was a new way to write a book, but it was what I needed to do last year as I was grieving.

As I was struggling in 2023, my crows found me. No matter what happened or how I felt, I could count on going on my walk and connecting with them. Crows are so consistent and it's one of their best traits. It even seems to be their preference to be consistent. I love them as if they are my beloved personal pets, all 10,000 Woodinville crows. So many crows in a tiny town of 14,000 people and 140 wineries… Maybe it's the small population paired with lots of outdoor dining that they like, where they can scrounge for discarded, spilled food left by tipsy patrons? Or the winery estates and farms and fields that they pick through during the day? The slow-flowing river and the parks where people are frequently picnicking? For whatever reason, they love it here.

I feel a lot of love for those around me… people, animals, trees and plants. A few months ago I noticed how quiet my house was, and I started talking to my (formerly withering, almost-dead) plant. He now has 3 new sprouts since I've started conversing with him. Hanging on by a thread for years, he is now thriving.

With my crows, I definitely needed them in the year after I lost my dog, but I know they didn't need me. Still, I don't feel like my love for them is ever wasted. I'm putting love out there, they are picking it up, and whatever they don't pick up just benefits me. Actually, I've always felt that intrinsically, the love we feel inside benefits us first, our mind and body and soul, before we can push it out into the universe. With absolutely no expectation of it coming back to me, since feelings have such an automatic, subconscious inception anyway, how could love ever be wasted?

Conclusion

One of my mottos in life, apparently, is to find something I love and then do that thing 1,000%. I've always been that way. Reading books, writing, watching films, studying languages, traveling, dogs, photos, on and on.

I know what I like, and I do those things. It makes me happy to be so in tune with my own interests and hobbies, things that bring me joy. And then after a while, these hobbies become a habit, a pattern. Like many people and animals, I am such a creature of habit, and I loved walking with my crows for 365 days (minus 2 days when I was out of town), through rain and snow and 90-degree weather and 12-degree weather, when I wasn't feeling well but still wanted to see them.

It is also a habit I will continue after these 365 days, maybe not every day, but as often as I can. My crows helped me through the roughest time of my life. I will forever be grateful to them for that, that they were a constant, consistent source of support whenever I needed it. Whenever my friends were busy, or when my family was out of town, I knew I could always see my crows on my walk. That's the thing with having 10,000 crows; you know there is always going to be at least one crow friend there waiting for you, waiting for a snack, wanting to say hello and join you on part of your walk. And walking with me for a minute, for an afternoon, is not unlike friendships that are part of our lives for a time but maybe not forever. Like a friend who enters into the river stream with us for a while, and then exits a little ways away.

"Thanks for being there on part of my journey."

My crows have been great friends to me. During our lives, we may interact with any number of beings: family, friends, animals, our Higher Power, acquaintances, community members. They all bring something to our lives, either great or small. And in most cases, we bring something to them as well.

There's a powerful scene in the movie "Ordinary People" that I think about quite often, almost subconsciously at this point, now that I walk with crows. In the scene, Mary Tyler Moore is sitting in the yard with Timothy Hutton, talking about his childhood and about a bird that used to hang out in their garage. MTM makes a "swooshing" sound and waves her hands, imitating the bird's wings when it flies away. It's an impactful scene as Pachelbel's Canon in D plays, and an overall fabulous (but highly emotional) movie.

I always hear that "swooshing" sound on my walk, as the crows fly above and beside me. It scared me the first couple times, but now I'm thrilled when I hear that sound. In the summer, I would see their shadow on the sidewalk in front of me, and it was another type of hide-and-seek game, looking up and seeing where they'd eventually landed. The crows are getting closer and closer day by day, month by month, as we feel more comfortable with each other. I love it; and if they wanted to get in my car and come home with me, I'd be happy.

One night I had a dream that I had adopted an injured corvid. He was huge, and probably a raven, not a crow. He was so cute; I loved him. When things from my life start showing up in my dreams, I know I'm all in. I'm definitely all in with crows.

I wasn't sure where these walks were going, my time with crows, but I have enjoyed what has happened between us over the past year. Maybe it was an opportunity for me to enrich my understanding and my life; it has been a truly magical time, and opened up my eyes to the ways other living creatures communicate with us. And, my crows helped me heal when I needed it most. For that, I will be forever grateful.

References

Andrei, M. (2023, April 18). *What do Crows Eat? from nuts and seeds to carrion and in between*. ZME Science. https://www.zmescience.com/feature-post/what-do-crows-eat/

Berman, R. (2020, September 29). *Crows are self-aware just like us, says New Study*. Big Think. https://bigthink.com/neuropsych/crows-higher-intelligence/

Birdfact. (2022, March 14). Baby Crows: All you need to know (with pictures). https://birdfact.com/articles/baby-crows

Black, H. (2013, September 1). *Crows show off their social skills*. Scientific American. https://www.scientificamerican.com/article/crows-show-off-social-skills/

Butler, O., Herr, K., Willmund, G., Gallinat, J., Kühn, S., & Zimmermann, P. (2020). Trauma, treatment and Tetris: video gaming increases hippocampal volume in male patients with combat-related posttraumatic stress disorder. Journal of psychiatry & neuroscience : JPN, 45(4), 279–287. https://doi.org/10.1503/jpn.190027

Hamilton, G. (2012, November 7). *Crows can distinguish faces in a crowd*. National Wildlife Federation. https://www.nwf.org/Home/Magazines/National-Wildlife/2013/DecJan/Animals/Crows-Recognizing-Faces

Hietanen, J. K. (2018, August 28). *Affective eye contact: An integrative review*. Frontiers in psychology. https://www.ncbi.nlm.nih.gov/pmc/articles/PMC6121038/

Insano, C. (2023, April 16). *Why do crows gift humans?*. My Bird Garden. https://mybirdgarden.com/why-do-crows-gift-humans/

King TV. (2020, October 30). *Almost live!: Seattle Summer*. YouTube. https://www.youtube.com/watch?v=rsP2LGal0gQ

Lancaster University. (2016, July 26). Driving, thinking, dreaming: Why motoring can be therapeutic. *ScienceDaily*. Retrieved April 29, 2024 from www.sciencedaily.com/releases/2016/07/160726094826.htm

Meinch, T. (2023, March 17). *The more we learn about Crow Brains, the more humanlike their intelligence seems*. Discover Magazine. https://www.discovermagazine.com/planet-earth/the-more-we-learn-about-crow-brains-the-more-humanlike-their-intelligence

MTM Enterprises. (1972). *The Bob Newhart Show* [Television show]. United States.

NBC. (1995). *Friends*. [Television show]. United States.

Nichols, S. (2023, November 10). *How good is a crow's eyesight?* Birdful. https://www.birdful.org/how-good-is-a-crows-eyesight/

Paramount Pictures. (1980). *Ordinary People* [Film]. United States.

Participant. (2013, August 6). *Why we hug so hard it hurts | the science of happiness*. YouTube. https://www.youtube.com/watch?v=ApoYwEeDNrc

Rabbitt, M. (2024, March 27). *15 Major Benefits of Walking*. Prevention.

https://www.prevention.com/fitness/a20485587/benefits-from-walking-every-day/

Rhodes, J. (2013, July 1). *Why do I think better after I exercise?*. Scientific American. https://www.scientificamerican.com/article/why-do-you-think-better-after-walk-exercise/

Samuel, S. (2021, July 23). *Jane Goodall reveals what studying chimpanzees teaches us about human nature.* Vox. https://www.vox.com/future-perfect/22585935/jane-goodall-chimpanzees-animal-intelligence-human-nature

Schulze-Makuch, D. (2021, February 10). *Crows are even smarter than we thought.* Smithsonian.com. https://www.smithsonianmag.com/air-space-magazine/crows-are-even-smarter-we-thought-180976970/

Starr, M. (2020, September 28). *Crows are capable of conscious thought, scientists demonstrate for the first time.* ScienceAlert. https://www.sciencealert.com/new-research-finds-crows-can-ponder-their-own-knowledge

TEDx. (2014, January 23). *Crows, smarter than you think | John Marzluff | tedxrainier.* YouTube. https://www.youtube.com/watch?v=0fiAoqwsc9g

Twentieth Century Fox. (1992). *Home Alone 2: Lost in New York* [Film]. United States.

Universal Pictures. (1963). *The Birds* [Film]. United States.

University of Washington. (2021, December 21). *A story of 10,000 crows: The nightly migration to UW Bothell Campus.* UW College of the Environment. https://environment.uw.edu/news/2021/12/a-story-of-10000-crows-the-nightly-migration-to-uw-bothell-campus/

University of Washington. (2024). *Faculty: John Marzluff.* College of the Environment.
https://environment.uw.edu/faculty/john-marzluff/

Walt Disney. (1966). *The Ugly Dachshund* [Film]. United States.

ABOUT THE AUTHOR

Katie Brotten is a Social Worker in the Seattle area. She enjoys spending time outdoors in nature, including going hiking and taking long walks. She loves animals of all kinds, especially dogs and crows. In her free time, Katie loves to write. *Worthy Caws* is her second book. Her first book was *Vinnie and His Weird Ear: Adventures with the dog who saved my life.*

Printed in Great Britain
by Amazon